Physical Ch
Perro d

(from the breed standard of the Club Español del Presa Canario)

Body: Longer than the height at the shoulder by about 20%. Wide chest, deep brisket level with elbows, with marked pectoral muscles. Dorso-lumbar line straight, ascending slightly to the loins. Well-arched rib cage, almost cylindrical. Loin straight, medium length and wide.

Color: All types of brindle, from very warm dark colors to gray or very light brown or blonde. Full range of fawn to sand-colored. In general, there are more or less long white markings on the chest. The mask is always dark and may extend around the eyes.

Tail: Set on high, flexible, strong at the root and tapering to the hocks. In action, elevated saber-like with the tip pointing forward but not curled.

Height at shoulder:
Males: 61 to 66 cms. (24 to 26 ins.).
Females: 57 to 62 cms. (22.5 to 24.5 ins.).

Hindquarters: Hindlegs powerful, straight when viewed from the side or front. Very muscular second thighs, unpronounced angles. Cat-like feet. Hocks low and neither sickle nor cow.

Weight: Average male: 45–57 kgs. (100–125 lbs.). Average female: 40–50 kgs. (88–110 lbs.).

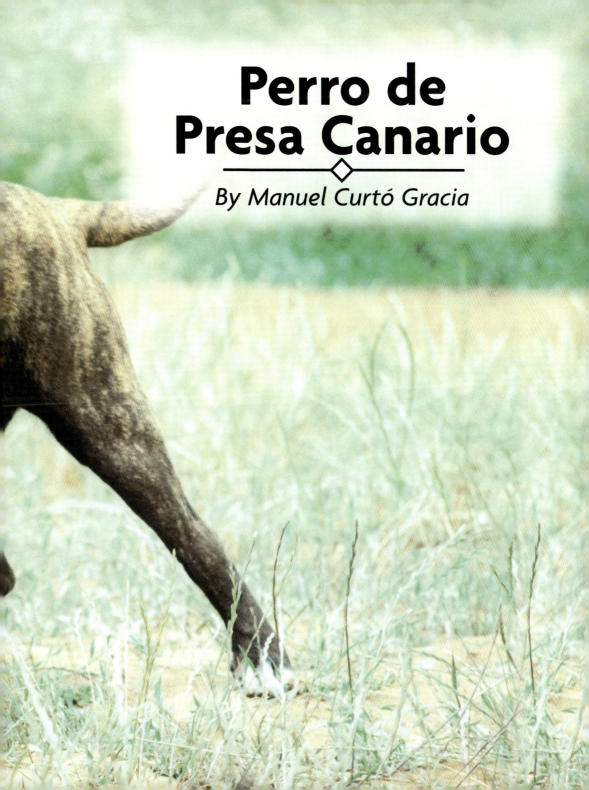

Perro de Presa Canario

By Manuel Curtó Gracia

Contents

KENNEL CLUB BOOKS® **PERRO DE PRESA CANARIO**
ISBN: 1-59378-331-0

Copyright © 2003, **2006** Kennel Club Books LLC
308 Main Street, Allenhurst, NJ 07711 USA
Cover Design Patented: US 6,435,559 B2 • Printed in South Korea

Photography by Isabelle Français
with additional photographs by:

Norvia Behling, T. J. Calhoun, Irena Curto, Carolina Biological Supply,
David Dalton, Doskocil, James Hayden-Yoav, James R. Hayden, RBP, Bill Jonas,
Dwight R. Kuhn, Dr. Dennis Kunkel, Mikki Pet Products, Phototake, Jean Claude Revy,
Dr. Andrew Spielman, Tim and Katheryne Stevenson and Alice van Kempen.

The publisher wishes to acknowledge the owners of the Presas in this book: Irena
Curto, Manuel Curtó Gracia, Juan de Dias, Dr. Antonio Gallardo,
Julie L. Goldenberg, Santiago Arteaga Gonzalez, Antonio Gulierez Hdeez,
David Meyer, Rosasara Dibba Madrid, Sr. Olejnik and Oscar Peralta Teixeira.

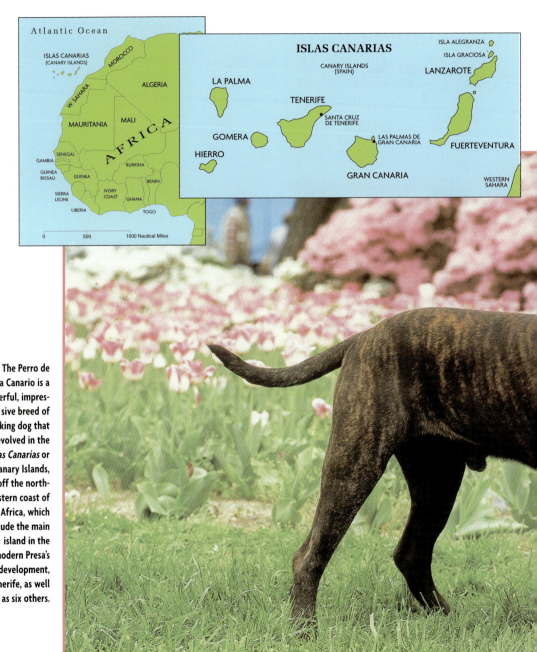

Atlantic Ocean

ISLAS CANARIAS
(CANARY ISLANDS)

MOROCCO

ALGERIA

W. SAHARA

MAURITANIA   MALI

SENEGAL

GAMBIA

GUINEA
BISSAU   GUINEA

SIERRA
LEONE   IVORY
COAST   GHANA

LIBERIA   TOGO

AFRICA

BURKINA

BENIN

0   500   1000 Nautical Miles

ISLAS CANARIAS

CANARY ISLANDS
(SPAIN)

ISLA ALEGRANZA

ISLA GRACIOSA

LA PALMA

TENERIFE

LANZAROTE

SANTA CRUZ
DE TENERIFE

GOMERA

HIERRO

LAS PALMAS DE
GRAN CANARIA

FUERTEVENTURA

GRAN CANARIA

WESTERN
SAHARA

The Perro de Presa Canario is a powerful, impressive breed of working dog that evolved in the *Islas Canarias* or Canary Islands, off the northwestern coast of Africa, which include the main island in the modern Presa's development, Tenerife, as well as six others.

HISTORY OF THE
PERRO DE PRESA CANARIO

The Perro de Presa Canario is becoming quite fashionable as more and more people are attracted to this powerful and trustworthy breed. As the breed has become more popular around the world, much has been speculated and written about these dogs, much of which immensely varies from the truth.

THE PRE-HISPANIC DOGS

The Canary Islands were first given that name by Plinio and Estacio Seboso, and it is thought that the name was taken from the big canines that were found on

The essence of the Presa Canario is exemplified by the breed's magnificent head and intense expression.

these islands at the times of the famous Juba expedition. Two of those first big dogs were taken as gifts to the King of Mauritania. Many dog fanciers interested in the dogs of the Canary Islands accept this historical reference. The etymology, though accepted by a large number of people, has found opposition with others.

There were never corpulent canines in the Canary Islands. Missionaries and historians from Bethencourt expressly mentioned in their descriptions of the island's fauna: "There are pigs, goats, sheep and wild dogs that look like wolves, although they are small." Juba, a philosopher and naturalist from this period, was the first to gather accurate information on the archipelago. Therefore, it is evident that since the days of this first world-renowned exploration of the

islands, they were named the Canary Islands. This was either after the *ingentis magnitudinis* canines cited by Plinio or perhaps for other reasons supported with different, perhaps more sound, criteria.

Considering this and other careful observations, new etymological theories, which we will briefly present here, emerged. Plinio purported that to the west of the islands, certain communities could be found under the name of Canaries. That was perhaps the reason that Ptolomeo used the name "Caunaria Extrema" for the Bojador Key. The question arises: Did these names derive from what had previously been the island of Canaria or, conversely, did the island borrow its name from those peoples and the African promontory? Whatever the answer, it is important to remember that there is a correlation between both designations.

Others believe that the island of Gran Canario borrowed its name from the word *canna*, related to the Canary euphorbia (officinal spurge), the ferula of the Latin people or bitter cane, which Juba knew well. He actually wrote a treaty about this vegetation and named it "Euforbio," after his doctor. In his writings from 1525, Tomás Nichols supports this hypothesis and adds, "I've heard from ancient inhabitants that the island was named like that (Canaria) after certain bitter cane that abundantly spreads throughout the country and from which a highly poisonous milk can be extracted." The island of Gran Canaria (Grand Canary) was also called Tamarán or Tamerán by its first inhabitants, the meaning of which seems to be "country of the brave" in their native tongue.

Nevertheless, if the word *Canaria* derives from *can* or *canna*, that is of no relevance to us now. The importance lies in the actual size of those two dogs, which, according to Plinio and Estacio Seboso, were taken to the King of Mauritania (Juba II). This, too, we will not be able to confirm.

Bontier and Le Verrier wrote the book *Le Canarien*. They were missionaries at the service of Jean de Bethencourt, who was the first conqueror of the Canary Islands. The book says that "in those islands there were dogs that looked like wolves, but smaller." This description matches with the canine remains found by archeologists in both Grand Canary and Tenerife. So far, no traces of dogs from before the conquest and colonization of the Canary Islands have been found on any of the other islands of the archipelago (Fuerteventura, Lanzarote, El Hierro, La Gomera and La Palma.) Therefore, we can infer that there were no dogs of this kind there.

Canine remains were found next to those of their masters in several sepulchral caves in Tenerife, but it was in the Necropolis of El Llano de Maja where a dog's skull was found next to the remains of its shepherd and surrounded by a complete set of funeral accessories. The skull was one of a small-sized dog with a short coat of a dark cream color and traces of mummification in some areas, according to the writings of Luis Diego Cuscoy, an archeologist and director of Tenerife's Archeological Museum.

Fray Alonso de Espinosa, born in 1543, lived among the last *guanches* in the south of Tenerife and wrote about the aboriginal dogs: "These dogs were mongrels or small yappers, which the

THE NAME "CANARY DOG"

The name "Canary Dog" is an anglicization of the original Spanish name for the breed, coined by American dog fancier Dr. Carl Semencic. The author has chosen not to propagate this name in this volume for the simple reason that there are five existing breeds of dog on the Canary Islands, not just the Perro de Presa Canario. Thus, "Canary Dog" does not accurately describe the Presa breed and should not be applied to these dogs.

natives called *cancha*." It is apparent to the author (and so far nobody has proved otherwise) that the dogs belonging to the native inhabitants of Grand Canary and Tenerife were small in size and became extinct some time long ago.

THE ANCIENT DOGS OF THE CANARY ISLANDS

The dogs of the Canary Islands, namely those of Tenerife, were first cited on September 3, 1515. The citation reads: "No person should have a dog inside his house or property and he should keep it tied up all day, and the pig shepherds can have a dog on their herds as long as it is not a Canary dog." Conquerors and their dogs are first cited together in November 1404, when Bethencourt's men (the first conquerors of the Canary Islands) went searching for the natives on Lanzarote: "And they have dogs with them." This reference does not inform us of the kind of dogs they kept, mastiffs, shepherding dogs or prey dogs (dogs used for hunting purposes, chasing and catching).

It is thus easy to conclude that the conquerors' dogs were of considerable size, suitable for guarding, defense and war, although there is no evidence proving that they were used for the capture of native Canary people. An uninformed author in recent times wrote that the natives used their dogs for the defense of the islands against conquerors. This author cannot find a single reference in any history of the Canary Islands that confirms this theory. We think it is pure invention, based on a flight of romance and fancy!

Prey dogs, herding dogs and hunting dogs are often cited in the statutes and agreements of the town halls of Tenerife and Fuerteventura from the 16th through 18th centuries. These dogs are referred to as wandering out of control through the countryside, inflicting damage on the cattle. There is a very detailed ordinance, dated February 5, 1516, which reads as follows:

"Related to the great damage that dogs inflict upon the cattle, major and minor, and such dogs belong to *pegueros* (pitch manufacturers), *almocrebes* (muleteers) and other people of poor living who take the dogs with them to their rides and hunting and stealing. Some of the dogs went off without their owners and others turned wild or feral, becoming worse than wolves. Thus it was ordered, on the third day, that everyone owning a dog was to kill it. However, this ordinance does not go against butchers' cutting and weighing meat, so that each of them can have two dogs at the meat market, keeping them tied up day and night and only letting them loose to chase the cattle. Likewise, the two dogs that are kept on the outskirts of town to kill the stray feral dogs (*asilvestrados*) should remain so that they can perform this needed task, provided that do not come into town and that they are trained, as they are in Adexe and Abona, where they are kept by councilman Pedro de Lugo."

No doubts that the butchers' dogs were used to chase and

catch prey, as likely were those belonging to Pedro de Lugo, which were trained to hunt wild dogs (*asilvestrados*). An ordinance of April 9, 1518 also refers to prey dogs: "A solution for the damage caused by wild dogs, of which there is at present a good deal, may rest in certain dogs kept by a gentleman. These dogs have killed many wild dogs, and their pelts are displayed in town hall. It would be fair to provide this man with good payment for his services, and entrust him as

The Presa was considered a butcher's dog in the olden days, as the term *presa* indicates a dog that was a catcher of cattle or a prey dog.

guardian. All cattle breeders should contribute their share and request that Valdés and Las Hijas support a just law to help alleviate this problem."

An ordinance dated February 20, 1523 reads: "And the dog's ordinance ought to be proclaimed since they are harmful and kill the cattle. Valdés said that no dog should be killed except those that are harmful. We should proclaim and keep the ordinance and assign Castellano and Gallinato to choose dogs suitable to kill the wild dogs."

Since the days of conquest and colonization, the Canary prey dogs became important for the services they offered to inhabitants. The people used the dogs to immobilize the cattle for the slaughter, to hunt wild dogs and, later, to guard and drive the cattle (this practice has only been carried out during the last few decades for the guarding of houses and farms).

In Fuerteventura, just like in Tenerife and the rest of the islands, prey dogs carried out the functions of chasing and catching wild dogs, as the uncontrolled *asilvestrados* still posed problems. An example of this appears in an agreement of Betancuria (Fuerteventura), dated October 21, 1624, which reads as follows: "The goat and sheep and cattle were damaged by the dogs, therefore, it is agreed that all people—in eight days—keep a dog each to watch over the house and kill any others. And this applies to both hunt and prey dogs..." In another agreement, dated August 16, 1630, we read, "Anyone owning prey dogs should notify the judicial system."

Fifteen years later, the general deputy, Sebastián de Betancor, demanded the killing of dogs on the island due to the great damage they caused. It was then agreed that "all neighbors, residents and inhabitants kill the dogs they owned, except one prey or hunting dog, which they can keep to watch over their houses, as long as it is tied up; the slaughter was to take place within eight days or else they will be charged with a 600-maravedi fine."

The author notes that there is no description of these prey dogs that the people from the Canary Islands appreciated so much. It is curious that there is no written documentation to give us a better idea of their appearance. All we know, from the agreements and ordinances dating from those years, is that these dogs were useful to men, but those records are all we have. There is not even any record of oral tradition regarding these dogs until more modern times.

It all leads the author to propose that (as a whole) those prey dogs resembled their Spanish bulldog ancestors. It is well known that, centuries ago, there were different kinds of prey dogs or bulldogs in Spain. Famous painters such as Velázquez, Goya, Corvasí, Castellanos, Branchard, Perea y Rojas and Pérez Villaamil immortalized some of these dogs in their works. Jose María de Cossío (1893–1977), author of *Los Toros Encyclopedia*, writes, "The dogs used for this purpose were the ones called *alanos*. They were a Spanish breed of prey dog, very strong and corpulent, with a big head, dropped ears (which are usually cropped to avoid further cuts or bites as they struggle to get hold of prey), flat nose and a long tail." Therefore, we theorize that there were different kinds of prey dogs in the Canary Islands, which all had the same use in the end.

This is all we have managed to find out about the "ancient" Canary dogs. Some Canary dog fanciers have tried, with or without actual documentation, to support and promote the hypothesis that certain strains of the ancient breed reached the 1970s. They have also said that, from that time on, the Presa Canario we know today was progressively shaped by means of cross-breeding the ancient strains with imported prey dogs.

EAR CROPPING

Ear cropping consists of surgically trimming the ear leathers and then training the ears to stand upright. Originally, cropping was done to prevent the ears from being bitten by prey, vermin or any adversary. With fighting dogs and terriers, cropped ears gave the opponent less to hang on to. Ear cropping also is considered important for cosmetic purposes, as it gives the dog a very smart look. In the US, dogs can be shown with cropped or natural ears, as is the case in most European nations. In the UK, however, ear cropping has been banned for years. American breeders concentrate on the stylish look of cropped ears, which they believe give the dog's head a more appealing, sharper look. In fact, at most shows in the US, it is more difficult to do top winning with a dog with natural ears, though some pet owners favor the uncropped look.

BRAIN AND BRAWN

Since dogs have been inbred for centuries, their physical and mental characteristics are constantly being changed to suit man's desires for hunting, retrieving, scenting, guarding and warming their masters' laps. During the past 150 years, dogs have been judged according to physical characteristics as well as functional abilities. Few breeds can boast a genuine balance between physique, working ability and temperament.

This statement (which could be so suggestive for nationalists, who defend the autochthonous) is by no means bearable. The only remains of those ancient dogs, which were brought to the Canary Islands by conquerors and colonizers from the Iberian Peninsula, are the Perro de Ganado Majorero (a type of cattle dog) and the Podenco Canario (a type of small sighthound). The former is a polyvalent relation of the mastiff and the wolf, very apt at guarding, defense and hunting, with certain inherited traits and behavior—in my belief—from ancient Canary prey dogs. I think that this could be the result of crossing with those prey dogs, which I am absolutely sure did take place, for whatever reasons. There are neither record nor remains left of the rest of the dog breeds introduced to the Canary Islands by the conquerors and colonizers.

"The most common dogs found on the islands were mastiffs, shepherd dogs, hounds, *perdigueros* or partridge-hunting dogs, molossers or mastiff-type dogs, ancient short-legged hunting dogs known as *pachones*, water dogs, bloodhounds, etc.," according to Viera y Clavijo in the 1760s.

I believe that it is extremely important to consider the cattle dog and its origins and evolution in time. Right now, nearly all of the attention is focused on the fashionable Presa Canario. However, if we are to analyze modern Presa Canarios, which derive from the aforementioned cattle dogs, we conclude that, without the cattle dog, there would not be any other dogs on the Canary Islands. Neither one can be studied without the other. To put it in other words: all prey dogs born in the Canary Islands without a significant part of their genes coming from those cattle dogs can neither be nor should they be considered true Perros de Presa Canario.

THE ENGLISH PREY DOGS

In 1982, I wrote an extensive article about the Canary prey dog, which was published in *El Día* daily newspaper in Tenerife. A year later, an abridged version appeared in *El mundo del perro* dog magazine (Madrid). In part, I wrote: "The English, who seem to have been the ones who brought a fondness for dog fighting to the Canary Islands, would have brought their mastiffs, which were already famous for being good fighters at the times of Caesar; the ruthless bull terriers, which were able, more at those times than now, to fight against and defeat dogs far bigger than themselves; the bullmastiffs, the bulldogs, etc."

I reached this conclusion without any research, as my passion for the subject matter was intense, though my knowledge of the history of the Canary Islands, where I live, was scarce. I knew nothing of the informative town-hall agreements and ordinances of Tenerife and Fuerteventura, where the diversity of dog breeds is repeatedly mentioned from the first years of the conquest and colonization of the islands.

Many dog breeds were brought to the islands from Spain, even after the conquest and colonization. The Spanish land-owning families, with social prestige and economic power, who were settled in the islands, continued importing dogs from the peninsula to maintain the Spanish breeds in the archipelago. This was confirmed in

The Podenco Canario is a living testament to the forebears brought to the Islas Canarias by Iberian conquerors. This rare sighthound is a small, lithe and swift working dog, similar to the better known Ibizan Hound and Pharaoh Hound.

the writings of Viera y Clavijo: "In 1764 rabies entered the islands through dogs brought from Spain and it was passed to others in Tenerife."

The indispensable trading of various domestic animals, first from Spain to the Canary Islands, became extensive after Columbus's second trip to America. There is plenty of documentation on this matter. Some dogs were even raised in the islands to be later used for the conquest of the New World.

By the end of the 15th century, "Juan Canario and his black dog were also famous in the Spanish island." However, we have not found a single document on the introduction of dogs or any other animal by the English into the Canary Islands.

There is no doubt that the islands were a source of interest for the British Crown in the 16th century, and that explains their constant pirating. "And it was all to do with the Canary insular border, which was then vital for the sailing of the Iberian fleet galleons and the Dutch and English privateering. It consti- tuted, together with the Azores archipelago, the perfect base for

A distant relation to the Presa, the Bullmastiff derives from English Mastiff stock that may have been influenced by the importation of Spanish bulldogs.

The author contends that the beautiful Spanish Mastiff, a powerful long-coated breed of flock guardian, is related to the English Mastiff through common descendants. This breed was used in crosses with the old-time Presas.

the 'race after Indies.' Besides this geographical and strategic significance, the Canary Islands offered other incentives to the 'adventurous merchants.' They marveled at the temperate weather conditions, the quality fruits harvested in their lands—perfect for exportation to the northern regions and to the Indies (sugar, molasses, wine)—and for the 're-exportation' of manufactured goods of European origin and uncontrollable destination."

Nevertheless, the Canary Islands and England traded sporadically, but relations between both kingdoms were extremely difficult. At the end of the 16th century, the constant pirate attacks of English sailors

The powerful Presa Canario shares like mastiff ancestors that were once called bandogs, referring to the fact that the dog needed to be tied. Tying a Presa defeats an owner's purpose of having an able-bodied guard dog.

occurred frequently on the Canary Islands. But trade is trade—the English needed Canary malmsey (a type of sweet wine), and the Canaries needed English products. A few English families settled down in La Laguna and La Orotava (Tenerife) as well as in El Real de Las Palmas (Grand Canary).

Another problem that made these trade relations and the settling of English families on the islands difficult was religion: "...the lists of grievances of the Inquisition, the documentation of counselorships and audiences comprise plenty of information on visitors and residents who either break the Spanish control or fall under sanctions. Such was

the case of the English merchants, who complain to the English Council of States for the mistreatment they claim to receive in the Canary ports by governors and inquisitors and for alleged crimes of trafficking and heresy."

Regarding the information available, it is very interesting to read about Thomas Nichols (by Alejandro Cioranescu), an English trade agent in the Canaries, who settled down in La Laguna in 1557. It is clear that, from the 16th to mid-19th century, commercial transactions between England and the Canary Islands were basically made through agents with residence (temporary, in most of the cases) on the islands. This was the case of Thomas Nichols, "who represented the interests of Anthony Hickman, Edward Castlyn and Thomas Lok." These English commercial intermediates did not provide the island with any domestic animals, neither cows, goats, pigs, horses nor dogs. By saying this, I do not mean that certain Englishmen did not come to the islands accompanied by their dogs, regardless of breed.

Relating the Canary prey dogs with certain English prey dogs such as the Bulldog, the Bullmastiff and the Bull Terrier has no solid basis. While I was the first author to make that mistake, others echoed me, no doubt influenced by the article I wrote in 1982. Regarding the dogs on the Canary Islands from the 15th through 18th centuries, there is no evidence of the practice of dog fighting in the islands before the 20th century. Its beginnings likely could have come from the English, though there is no solid basis to assert that either. Worthy of note is that in the Canaries (from the 1900s to about the 1950s), large feasts were held where mutton fights were as popular as those of dogs (not to mention cockfighting, which has reached our present day). As betting was not a practice in the Canaries, these fights did not resemble the ones carried out in England.

The most common types of dogs seen on the Canary Islands were prey dogs, cattle or shep-herd dogs, bulldogs, molossers, water dogs, hounds, blood-hounds, partridge-hunting dogs, *pachones*, etc. It is apparent that all of these breeds are typical of the breeds seen in Spain and could be found scattered throughout the peninsula.

Likewise, the author has written on another occasion that the English took various dogs from the Canary Islands back to Spain and the Iberian Peninsula. The English imported bulldogs from Spain at different times— some of these imports at end of the 19th century are well documented, including mastiffs, different partridge-hunting breeds and podencos (such as the

Bravery and confidence brim in the veins of today's descendants of the early fighting breed of the Canary Islands. The modern Presa Canario, as represented by this dog photographed in Tenerife, is the "purebred" descendant of the ancient breed once found on the Canary Islands.

Ibizan Hound from the Balearic Islands, from which the Pharaoh Hound is a partial descendant). The English Mastiff is related to the Spanish Mastiff, or so it seems, as are the Bulldog and Bullmastiff. The English Pointer, the English Setter, the Cocker Spaniel and the Irish Setter are descendants of Perdiguero de Burgos and the Perdiguero Navarro, the Spanish partridge pointers, as are many other spaniel breeds in the world.

Reverend M.B. Wynn, the well-respected breeder, author and judge, tells us in his book, *History of the Mastiff*, which was published in 1886, that Mr. Lukey (1804–1882) was the most influential breeder of his time. He joined the Mastiff fancy after seeing an impressive, beautiful black dog of this breed, being walked by a servant through the streets of London. The dog belonged to the Marques of Hertford. Mr. Lukey bought a brindle bitch with a docked tail and cropped ears to mate with the dog of the Marques. The result was "Yarrow," an extra-ordinary bitch, which was the foundation of Lukey's breeding line. Later on, when the bitch reached adulthood, she was mated with a reddish dog, named "Couched," an unbeatable fighter. Rev. Wynn believes that this dog was a Bulldog from Spain. Descendants from this

mating were present in most of the breeding lines of the turn of the century.

With the abolition of the Inquisition on July 15, 1834, trade relations between England and the Canary Islands went back to normal. It was from the second half of the 19th century on that the biggest ports of the Canaries in Santa Cruz de Tenerife and La Luz in Las Palmas de Grand Canary became shelters, points of relief and provisioning for the brigantines of diverse nationalities. The British brigantines always stood out for their tonnage, arching and operations. By the end of the century, all the wealth of the Canaries had come from the ports; they were built to satisfy the charcoal-burning capacities of the vessels in transit between continents.

At least Tenerife and Grand Canary escaped the social and economic lethargy in which they had been immersed for a century. It is fair to add that the existence of British firms on the bay of the islets (Grand Canary) and on the maritime façade of Santa Cruz de Tenerife was not limited to merely mediating between ports of embarkation and those of final destination. The English in the Canary Islands were, together with some pioneers from the islands, the vanguards of the new crops for exportation. The main

Some of the ancient *perros de tierra* looked more like the Perro de Presa Mallorquin (also known as the Caò de Bou). This modern breed is not very well known outside Spain, though it is an impressive Spanish bulldog breed.

The Dogue de Bordeaux, a strong bulldog-mastiff breed of France, was used in limited numbers by modern breeders to recreate the Presa Canario.

crops were cochineal, which is a scarlet dye used for food coloring, between 1860–1880, and banana and tomato from the end of the century to the Golden Age, 1910–1930.

It was only after the abolition of the Holy Office (Inquisition) that non-Catholic foreigners could finally settle down in the Canaries. However, do not think that the English came to the Canaries in large numbers. Many of the families returned to England in due time, explaining why there are few British descendants in the islands, as few of them mixed with the local inhabitants. Their language,

traditions, education, culture, religious beliefs and peculiarities made them live in their own world in the islands. That was the way it was in those times, and how it still is today. However, it is true that with the boom of the tourist industry, the Canary Islands have become much more cosmopolitan in recent years.

THE CANARY DOG FROM 1900 TO 1970
In the early 1970s, I decided to write a book about Perros de Presa in the Canaries and, thus, began compiling data and photographs and searching for

these Presas throughout the Canary archipelago. The task was not easy. Soon after I began, I gave up the project. There were not any Presas; there was none left and no people who liked to breed them. The truth is that prey dogs and dog fights had already become part of the past. I did find a few mongrels, which locals called Perros de Presa; first in Grand Canary, then in Tenerife. It is clear that those mongrels, just like the old prey dogs, were not called Canary Dogs. They were called plainly "Perros de Presa," and that name was used for all dogs resembling prey dogs, foreign or local, crossed or not. The ones I saw in those years were mongrels of English Bulldogs, Great Danes and/or Boxers.

I wandered and wandered around the islands, except for La Palma, which I don't know why I never got to visit. I interviewed a number of old-timers who had had prey dogs, and the results in all cases were disappointing. There were no Presas anymore like the ones that existed previously on the islands. Many people apologized for not having any true Presas like the ones that could be found before. I asked every person for photographs to see what the dogs they talked about really looked like. There I was in search for my mythical dog, from town to town, from house to house, from person to person, but nothing came out of my search.

The first written documents about Presas were published in 1976 in the *El Día* daily newspaper (Tenerife). The first standard project appears in *Doggy People* magazine in the same year. By this, I mean that there is no written record whatsoever of the dogs before this year; therefore, whatever I found out was through interviewing the old-timers who had something to say about the dogs.

I asked Francisco Saavedra y Bolaños to recall what he could about the earlier Perros de Presa; his answers follow the questions and are in quotation marks. Can you remember the first fight between Presa dogs you ever saw? "Yes, the boy with the brown coat and the black dog called Negro. I was fourteen years old. Negro was a very brave dog. That was in 1928." How did those dogs look? "They were not the old Presa dogs." Who organized the fights? "Fights were not organized. You had a dog, I had a dog and we put them to fight whenever we wanted." Was there money betting in the fights? "No, there wasn't. We did it to see which dog was the best. That was all." With which foreign breeds were local dogs crossed in those years? "Bull Terriers, Bulldogs, Great Danes."

Why did you cross them? "To get a more beautiful and better prey-catcher dog." Can you remember the last typical Perro de Presa? Could you, please, describe it? "The *perro de tierra* (earth dog) was big, with long flews, big head and chest. I was four years old or five when I saw two of them. People said that they were the real Presa dogs. The ones I saw were a male and a bitch. They were siblings. They belonged to Marcos Mendoza and Antonio Enríquez." Could you tell me how the Presa and the earth dog differed in those years? "The Presa dog had a big head, but it wasn't that big and its chest was wide. And the earth one looked more like the 'Majorero' cattle dog, but maybe bigger. It was the sort of dog which was used for driving the cattle."

Salvador Hernández Rodríguez was born in 1922 and witnessed a dog fight for the first time in 1949. I asked him which dogs were his best prey dogs?, and he replied, "My best prey dog was Nerón. The dog had some foreign blood. Then came Negrito, a black dog. And Merenes. For this one I paid 1400 pesetas. It was a great dog. In those years you could have bought a yoke of oxen for that money." Which foreign breeds were crossed with the local dogs in those years? "Bulldog, Bull

Terrier, Great Dane. But such crossbreeding depreciated the dogs' value." Why did you cross them? "To make them bigger, we used the Great Dane; to make them fearless, the Bull Terrier; and to make them wider and better prey-catchers, we used the Bulldog. But it was a mistake." Can you remember the last typical Perro de Presa? "Yes, Molone, a male, out of a bitch that belonged to the Count de la Vega Grande. It was a dark brindle dog of approximately 100 pounds or 45 kilos. I won three trophies with that dog in the exhibitions that were organized by the town hall. There were exhibitions for dogs, cows and goats. That dog had a big head and a wide chest."

Demetrio Trujillo Rodríguez was born in 1928. At the age of eight, he saw the first Presa dog fight. I asked him which foreign breeds were crossed with our local dogs in those years, and he answered, "They were mated with Bulldogs, Bull Terriers and Great Danes." Why did you cross breeds? "Because the result was more powerful dogs with wider chests, bigger heads." Can you remember the last typical Presa you saw? "I do not remember the Perro de Presa. In those years, all dogs had already been crossed with foreign breeds." Could you tell me the difference between a *perro de tierra* and a Presa dog?

"I cannot tell you, since I never saw a real prey dog here."

Of all Presa dog owners or *preseros*, old men all of them, whom I interviewed, the most interesting to me was Polo Acosta y Acosta. No doubt he was a real character! He was born in the high side of La Esperanza (Tenerife), very close to where I've lived for over 20 years. He knew a lot about local cows and goats, cockfighting, Presa dogs and *pechadas* (dog fights with Presas). Furthermore, Polo Acosta was an excellent Canary-pole player and an expert in Canary wrestling, founder of the Tinguaro and Calana teams.

I visited Polo Acosta at his home in Boquerón many times in the 1980s. "Yes, Don Manuel, there are no Presas like the ones there used to be," he told me in frustration. He told me stories about dogs and dog fights from the days of his youth. He spoke about Marruecos, a dog that Juan el Marchante from La Palma brought for him. "The best Presa dog I've ever had in my life—he had no rival. Marruecos died tied

The mighty Fila Brasileiro, a fierce and fearless working dog of Brazil, was used in the recreation of the Presa Canario breed in Gran Canario only.

to a big chestnut tree, close to where you live, up there in El Ortigal. We used to live there, in that little house, now covered with bramble bushes, which collapsed many years ago. Yes, the dog was the son of a Bull Terrier with a *perro de tierra* bitch."

According to what Polo Acosta told me, he never got to see the ancient Presa dogs. All of his dogs were results of crossbreeding with Great Danes, English Bulldogs, Bull Terriers, Spanish Mastiffs or local cattle dogs. Next to the municipal slaughterhouse in Santa Cruz, he said, there was what we call a dog stable or barracks, where dogs of different breeds, belonging to different owners, were kept for crossbreeding to produce dogs to be used in the fights. It was from there that the best Presa dogs in Tenerife came. "Oh, yes! Mocho, owned by Domingo Palma; Valiente, owned by Santos; Verga and many, many others. I had many Presa dogs besides Marruecos. I had Corbato, Quebrao, Cuidao, Porqué, Nilo, Chumbo."

From the beginning of the 20th century up to the 1940s, Presa dog trafficking among the islands was a frequent practice. People fond of dog fighting were always looking for the unbeatable dog and, for that purpose, they kept crossing different breeds.

None of the old dog breeders I interviewed from the early 1970s to the late 1990s knew about modern breeds such as the Mastiff, the Bullmastiff, the American Pit Bull Terrier, the American Staffordshire Terrier, the Staffordshire Bull Terrier, the Neapolitan Mastiff or the Dogue de Bordeaux, nor had they even heard about them. The last interview I did was with Manuel Caporal, from Los Campitos, Tenerife, and Angel Goya from the same village.

THE PRESA DOGS FROM 1970 TO THE PRESENT

After the previous analysis, I dare to assert, without fear of mistake, that in 1975 there were no Presa dogs in the Canaries. I am not talking about the ones from centuries ago, which probably became extinct in the early years of the 20th century. No, I'm talking about those Presa dogs used for dog fighting that resulted from later crosses with *perros de tierra*, cattle dogs, English Bulldogs, Great Danes, Bull Terriers and Spanish Mastiffs, among other breeds.

Therefore, the modern Perros de Presa Canario are direct descendants of certain crosses, mostly with other prey dogs. These crossings have been carried out since 1975 (first in Grand Canary and then in Tenerife). The breeds used were

the following: the Neapolitan and English Mastiffs, the English Bulldog, the Bull Terrier, Staffordshire Bull Terrier, the Bullmastiff, the Great Dane, the Rhodesian Ridgeback (a few were used and only in Grand Canary), the Perro de Ganado Majorero (especially in Grand Canary), the Spanish Mastiff, the American Staffordshire Terrier, the American Pit Bull Terrier, the Dogue de Bordeaux (not many), the American Bulldog (not many), the Fila Brasileiro (not many and only in Grand Canary) and others that we consider inconsequential.

At first, these crosses were aimed at producing dogs in better shape for fighting (in Grand Canary, but not so much in Tenerife, where, except for a few cases, there were serious attempts to breed Presa dogs for companionship and guarding). But, with time, and due to the unpopularity and unavoidable clandestine nature of dog fights, the initial enthusiasm receded so much so that today we can say, just like in the early 1970s, that dog fights are part of the past. Today the Perro de Presa Canario is bred and selected for guarding and defense purposes only.

THE TRUE ORIGINS OF THE MODERN PRESA CANARIO
There are likely 500 breeds of dog throughout the world, only 330 of which are recognized by the Fédération Cynologique Internationale (FCI), the world's largest registry. Many dog breeds have been studied and promoted, and there are thousands of books about the more popular of these breeds. The author purports that, despite what most breed books say (or fail to say), all breeds derive from free crossing. Later on, by means of a process of selection and endogamy (the custom of mating only within the confines of a given community or region), these dogs have "evolved" into pure breeds. Hiding the true origins of modern dog breeds is a consequence of the concept of what constitutes a pure breed, formulated by the founders of breed clubs, which have proliferated throughout the world since the late 19th century. Dog shows provide another reason to conceal a breed's true genesis, as without dog breeds, dog shows are meaningless.

This matter has concerned me for some time. When I became interested in the origins of the Doberman Pinscher, the Bullmastiff, the Neapolitan Mastiff, the Dogue de Bordeaux— just to mention a few—I noticed that it was impossible discover the true origins of these breeds; that is, which breeds or dogs had played roles in forming the modern breeds we know today.

Experts currently working for dog clubs have told me that the origin of a breed is irrelevant and is not something to be concerned about. What really is important is the breed that results. This approach to dog breeds leaves me perplexed. It is maybe because I am too inquisitive. It is my belief that knowing the past, the origins, the history or genesis of a people, culture, dog breed, etc., helps us to understand ourselves better, to understand our culture better, to understand our dogs better

(whatever breed), individual to individual.

That is why I began to write about the Presa Canario in the mid-1970s, before the dog was considered as a separate breed. My first writings, published in *El Día* newspaper, *Doggy People* magazine and *Dog World*, are the first written references to the Presa Canario as a "breed," though at the time the Presa was not even an established purebred.

The Neapolitan Mastiff was crossed with existing Presas to revive the breed. The Neo, as this breed is called by its followers, is a massive, formidable mastiff that can weigh as much as the English Mastiff (over 200 lbs).

Several years later, in 1982, the newly formed breed club in Spain (Club Español del Presa Canario) sought official recognition and set out to convince the world that the Presa was indeed a breed. Of course, the board members knew that unless the Presa was recognized as an extant breed, the Spanish Royal Canine Society would never grant admission to the Perro de Presa Canario.

To this end, the Club Español del Presa Canario drew up a "standard" for the Presa Canario, based on the descriptions of those elderly men who had once owned the dogs. The club was determined to convince the Spanish Royal Canine Society as well as the Spanish and Canary Island people that such a breed did in fact still exist.

The newly devised breed standard described the Presa as a medium-sized dog, rather longer than tall, with the croup higher than the withers. The Presa should have a large head with well-developed jaws, a barely visible stop, big oval-shaped eyes with a human-like expression and full dentition in a scissors bite (excessively undershot is considered a defect). Massive and robust, with a compact, strong body, the Presa possesses a wide chest, ample rib cage, strong limbs, moderately angulated hindquarters and well-angulated forequarters.

The standard also describes the Presa's temperament: always vigilant, very observant as a watchdog, uses its voice with reserve, self-confident, brave, with apparent territorial guarding instincts. The dog is never shy, insecure or irritable unless provoked. The Presa's gait is described as long strides at an unhurried pace, like that of a lion; an enduring gait over longer distance and a fast gallop in short distances. The dog should be able to drive cows to the pasturelands or control them when they resisted and return them to the stable.

This standard essentially describes an imaginary dog, and none of the Perros de Presa Canario in the islands even vaguely resembled this picture of perfection. Thus began the lofty endeavor to re-create a Presa that possessed these ideal features.

The old-timers explained that Presas in the old days had been crossed with Great Danes, Bulldogs, Bull Terriers, "Majorero" cattle dogs or other similar individuals. They were also crossed with dogs that were common on all the islands, which people called *perros de tierra*, as well as with Spanish Mastiffs. The crossings were done only to develop better dogs for the *pechadas* (the name given to dog fights in the Canaries). This limited breeding plan had no eye on conformation; it was aimed solely at obtaining a dog that could fight tirelessly. Dog fighters disdained the *pateros* (the name given to dogs that would merely bite their opponents in the legs and did not hold onto their opponents). The desirable Presa bit its opponent in the throat and would not let go. The ideal dog of the past was, then, the one that put its opponent down with only one bite, which could last 15 to 20 minutes, sometimes longer.

Breeding to meet the ideal set forth in the standard was to be neither an easy nor a fast job. While the pursuit of perfection and idealism are human follies, this pursuit did indeed bring about some reality. The two-faceted pursuit began: to promote the concept of the purebred Presa Canario through the media in Tenerife and the dog press, and to produce an actual Presa Canario to live up to the description that was being publicized.

That is how the fondness and enthusiasm for the Presa first started on and beyond the Canary Islands.

Some Canary Island natives began to participate in the nearly non-existent and forgotten sport of *pechadas* and became dedicated to breeding dogs for the purpose of fighting (mainly in Grand Canary). However, thankfully, the majority of people interested in the Presa intended to use the dogs as companions and guardians for their homes and properties.

Today, *pechadas* are quite rare in the Canary Islands. Nonetheless, only a small percentage of the people promoting the companion Presa concentrate on the health, temperament and function of the dogs. These dedicated fanciers, the author among them, place emphasis on the Presa's dependability as a companion dog, especially with children, and its ability to defend the home and act boldly when called upon to protect his family. The focus of the other fanciers was breeding strictly for conformation, the same kind of philosophy that has rendered many of the popular working breeds practically functionless.

The modern Presa Canario is a handsome, functional guard and companion animal.

CHARACTERISTICS OF THE
PERRO DE PRESA CANARIO

PHYSICAL CHARACTERISTICS

The Perro de Presa Canario is officially described today as a medium-sized dog with a straight profile. It looks rough and well proportioned. Mesomorphic, its body is longer than tall, and bitches are slightly longer than males. The breed possesses a solid, square head, with a wide skull. The upper lips cover the lower lips, and the pigmentation of the lips, eye rims and nose is black. The Presa possesses strong teeth, wide at base and generally well set; chestnut-colored, medium-sized eyes and high-set ears.

The neck is cylindrical, well muscled and covered with thick, loose, elastic skin. There should be a double dewlap, though this is not excessive. The chest is wide, the rib cage ample, the abdomen moderately withdrawn. The forequarters should be aligned perfectly, with wide, strong bones and accentuated angulation; this guarantees good cushioning and powerful stride. The front feet are described as "cat feet."

The hindquarters are powerful and muscular, with moderate angulation and correct alignment. The hind feet, also "cat feet," are slightly longer than the front feet. The tail is high-set. The skin should be thick and elastic, with a coat of short and rather rough hair, with no undercoat. Brindle, fawn and black coat colors are acceptable; each of these is generally seen with a black mask.

The general appearance of a Presa Canario is one of extraordinary power, especially suited to guard and defense work as well as the traditional purpose of driving cattle.

TEMPERAMENT AND OWNER SUITABILITY

The Presa possesses a steady disposition and a noble, calm bearing, though he distrusts strangers. He is an accomplished fighter and has a deep, chilling bark, well suited to warning suspicious strangers of his intentions and abilities to inflict harm if necessary.

While the Presa is a bold and powerful dog, he does not require a specific type of owner, provided his keeper is a caring, responsible dog person. The Presa is very

The Presa has a steady, noble disposition, but he does not trust strangers. Never approach an adult Presa that you do not know. The intimidating stare says it all.

A naturally talented guard dog, the Presa Canario requires no special training to become an ideal protector. He does require basic obedience training and a strong bond with his family.

wondrous attributes in spades.

It is clear that the heavier dogs (from 110–130 lbs. or about 50–60 kgs.) are not appropriate for exercises requiring a great deal of agility. No Presa has been selected for "circus acts," so you cannot expect a Presa to perform like a Poodle or Border Collie.

The Presa is indeed an ideal family dog, as in the home he is quiet, affectionate and sociable, invariably delighting in the company of children. The breed's calm disposition makes it ideal for life in a variety of settings, including a city apartment, a house with a yard or a large country estate. The breed's adaptability also includes changes in the weather, as the Presa does not mind excessively warm or cold climates.

As for children, who deserve special mention, they are the ones who benefit most from contact and friendship with dogs. Most children love dogs, and dogs love children. The Presa is ideal for children. He feels devotion for them. He is quiet and lets children play with him. The Presa adores children and the elderly alike. Maybe he sees them, somehow, as more vulnerable.

smart and extremely watchful. An owner with experience in training dogs has an advantage, as the Presa learns quickly. Most Presas have a natural aptitude for training and are capable of learning most any discipline, including herding, Schutzhund, obedience, agility, protection work, etc. Of course, the author must stress that *properly bred Presas from responsible breeders* possess these

TRAINABILITY OF THE PRESA CANARIO

The ideal Presa lives among his human family, without any special training, without causing the family problems or grief. He should know how to guard his family and defend his territory, protecting his owners whether he is with them at home or out for a walk. The author says "without any special training," although that does not mean that the puppy, like your own child, does not require basic lessons on how to behave properly. Presas do not respond to disciplinary training techniques, so proceed with your Presa's obedience training in a fair and consistent manner.

If you are so inclined to train the Presa on your own, without obedience classes or the help of a professional trainer, you will find that he is an excellent, attentive student. You will find the task of training your dog entertaining, enriching and rewarding. Reading books about training is a good idea or, if you are completely inexperienced in dog training, you should seek the assistance of an experienced professional. While the Presa is a trainable, intelligent dog, he is also a powerful, confident animal that can become dangerous if not sensibly trained.

The sensible training of the Perro de Presa Canario, unfortu- nately, has eluded many delusional dog trainers in recent years. These alleged dogmen are seeking to make the Presa, a naturally protec- tive and powerful dog, into a superdog, an unyielding biting machine. This is not a rational course to take with training a

Gentle, patient and tolerant, the Presa is an ideal family dog, well suited for a home with children. Responsible parents purchase only properly bred, well socialized and sound Presas to share their homes and lives with their children.

Presa, and your dog will not thrive if you attempt to program him to be a vicious man-stopping attack dog. The Presa is a down-to-earth working dog, capable of many tasks, but not prepared to overcome impossible comic-book obstacles drawn by obsessive trainers. The Presa requires a real owner, not one who is trying to cast his dog in a Hollywood action film.

Just as the American Pit Bull Terrier and American Bulldog, as well as the Fila Brasileiro, Rottweiler, Neapolitan Mastiff and Doberman Pinscher, were once the focus of irresponsible trainers, today they are looking toward the Presa Canario, which has been ineptly described as a "giant Pit Bull," to satisfy their warped cravings.

THE PRESA'S POTENTIAL— AN ANECDOTE

"Without any special training," the Presa is an excellent guard and defender, but has the poten-tial to be far more than just a protection dog. The author wishes to share the following anecdote to illustrate the Presa's versatility and abilities:

This story, which took place over 20 years ago, begins with Chelo, a bricklayer from La Gomera in the Canaries, who kept his Presa tied on his property on a 3-foot chain. In time, Chelo tired of the Presa and gave him to a farmer named Rosendo, who was very fond of local cows called *bastas*. Useful for plowing and cart pulling, these cows are also good dairy cows, capable of providing enough milk for the family as well as to sell at market.

Rosendo is rather a short man, who always wears a dark felt hat with a thick brim. He welcomes visitors with a kind of chronic displeasure, seemingly eyeing his visitors with a sour face. The first time I visited him, he already had Chelo's dog, which was lying there, chainless, well looked after and alert.

"Come in, *hombre*, come in, the dog is not going to do you any harm. He is well mannered and has learned a lot since he's been here," Rosendo said to me, without getting up from the corner on the floor, where he was sitting on top of a pile of un-ripened corn, which he had recently cut "for the cows."

The dog couldn't do a thing when Rosendo had gotten him from Chelo, but Rosendo had had plenty of time to teach the dog. The first thing he did when he brought the dog into the house was to bathe him. "Dogs like to be bathed," Rosendo told me. "Believe me; at the beginning they struggle, but they get to like it. After that I fed him, by hand, so that he could get to know me and accept me. It is not that he was not well fed before, not at all, but he did look a little bit thin and hungry and you must take advantage of that. For the dog to be a useful dog, we have to feed him with our own hands (at least, once in a while).

"Once he has finished eating, it is best to pet him and talk to him. I always do that. Look at him! He looks like a human! Can you see the way he looks at us? He knows that we are talking about him. Dogs are very smart, and they think, in their own way, but they do. And they suffer if one treats them badly. Did you know that dogs never do anything to upset humans? Oh, no, dogs are not mean like humans!"

To make a long story short, as they say, Rosendo, little by little, taught his dog to hold a coin with the nose to the wall. He put it against one of the walls of the cows' stable and told the dog, "Hold it there, don't drop it. Do you understand?" And the dog stayed there, happy like I've never seen any other before, holding the coin with the tip of his nose, until Rosendo said to him, "Drop it now, boy, that's enough. My friend now knows how smart you are!" And then the dog stepped away from the wall, dropping the coin to the floor. "Now bring it to me, boy, don't leave it there," Rosendo said to the dog, and the dog picked up the coin from the floor and took it to his master.

DOGS, DOGS, GOOD FOR YOUR HEART!

People usually purchase dogs for companionship, but studies show that dogs can help to improve their owners' health and level of activity, as well as lower a human's risk of coronary heart disease. Without even realizing it, when a person puts time into exercising, grooming and feeding a dog, he also puts more time into his own personal health care. Dog owners establish more routine schedules for their dogs to follow, which can have positive effects on their own health. Dogs also teach us patience, offer unconditional love and provide the joy of having a furry friend to pet!

More useful than holding a coin with his nose, Rosendo also taught the dog to carry the hoe in his mouth from one end of the field he was plowing to the other. When the plow's teeth got filled with wet soil, he said to the dog, "Bring me the hoe," and the dog ran for the hoe, returning with it, with his tail wagging happily the whole while.

"These dogs feel happy if you keep them busy," Rosendo told me, "I think this animal had never seen a hoe before moving into my house; however, look how he carries it now. He doesn't get tired. He likes it, believe me, he does; but listen, don't you think that I've forced him to learn all these things I've taught him by playing. If I give him a scythe, he will carry it all the same. Even if he sees me carrying it, he comes to me for me to give it to him.

"When I go to buy cigars, he always goes with me. He walks freely, no lead, walking happily by my side. Now when the salesman hands me the cigar box, he sits there and looks at me for me to give it to him. And even if I give him a bag with something I have bought inside it, he carries it too. He never leaves it behind. Nobody can take it away from him.

"He feels very threatened when someone tells him, 'Give me that!' and he growls at the person, looking very annoyed. He knows that the parcel belongs to his master, who feeds, bathes, pets and talks to him as if he were a human being. He understands me, and beware! Anyone thinking about raising a hand to me or threatening me should give it a second thought."

No trainer ever taught Rosendo's talented Presa. The dog never received any guidance in guarding or defense. But when I visited Rosendo, the dog would not let me in until his master stepped outside to see who was looking for him. As soon as Rosendo appeared, the dog adopted a different behavior— he just rested there, watching and listening to us. "He is a very reasonable dog," Rosendo said, "only he cannot speak."

There were many Presas like Rosendo's decades ago in the Canary Islands. It is a shame that these dogs do not exist here as they did in the past. The author believes the reason for the dogs' becoming neglected is that their utility to the people's agrarian lives dwindled away. The Presas were raised in close contact with their families and thrived on that interaction and the constant activity in the field. The dogs were true parts of the families and traveled with the families to the market and everywhere they went.

In order for a Presa to thrive in today's busy world, owners must commit to involving their dogs in their lives and not leave them home alone for eight hours or more each day. The Presa is a very grateful dog who learns quickly and can provide his owners with great satisfaction provided the owners are available to him. Keep your Presa active and involved, and he will become a most remarkable companion animal and protector.

THE RESPONSIBILITY OF PRESA FANCIERS

Every person who dares call himself a breeder knows how difficult it is to breed good dogs, regardless of the breed. Breeding Presas is—I would say—a double challenge. Approximately three decades of breeding and selection is not much time. Had the modern Perro de Presa Canario been based on existing dogs from the Canary Islands, the task would have been a thousand-fold easier. The Presa was not "revived" or "restored," it was "recreated."

More than a few aficionados—many of whom are breeders—regard speaking about the breed's true origin as taboo, an unforgivable mistake. I do not think so. Only with actual knowledge of the origins of the breed—the dogs that were used and the different breeds that were crossed—will breeders be able to follow a proper course in the shaping of this new and marvelous breed.

The serious, competent and responsible breeder needs deep,

thorough knowledge of the raw materials with which he is working. This knowledge could be of great help to shape his breeding program. Without those indispensable tools, a breeder cannot devise a dog that will breed "true." Without breeding true to type, there is no breed. A breed must be uniform in type, conformation, genetic material, temperament and behavior.

A breed is a genetic pattern, evident when puppies resemble their parents, in all senses, genera-

Active owners only, *por favor.* Keep your Presa busy and he will be a happy companion dog. This is a remarkable athlete, capable of any task you set before him.

tion after generation. Dog breeds have their origins, but they are never complete. They all evolve, due to continuous breeding and selection processes, feeding, adaptation to the environment, weather conditions, etc. In every epoch, tastes, fashions and necessities have made breeds evolve in one way or another, for better or for worse.

The Presa type is still being fixed, and breeders must take positive steps towards breeding typical Presas by selecting dogs with correct conformation, a stable character, balance, a brave and smart personality and a natural guarding instinct. Shaping a healthy and functional breed is not an easy job. That is why a large number of breeders is concerned about the "material" to be used in reproduction. The correct morphology (skull-face proportion, height at the withers, length, alignment, compactness, coat color, etc.) and the psychological balance are factors to consider in the reproduction of the Presa.

The breeding and selection of the Presa play a very significant role in society. In addition to the breed's traditional uses— shepherding, hunting, guarding— today the Presa also provides quality companionship to his master, works as a therapy dog, visiting hospitals and nursing homes, and serves as an assis- tance dog for the handicapped, as a guide to the blind and a hearing dog for the deaf.

HEREDITARY CONCERNS IN THE PRESA
One of the biggest concerns facing breeders is hip dysplasia, a hereditary condition that affects many large-breed dogs. Research has shown the condition can also be "aggravated" by the environ- ment, so breeders must be aware of this when rearing puppies. Among the contributing factors are poor feeding, lack of space for exercise, strenuous exercise for young developing pups, slippery surfaces in the dam's whelping pen, etc. The Presa puppy needs enough space to grow strong. A few square yards of floor space is not enough, unless he is frequently taken out to the countryside so that he can walk and run. Given the space to do so, a puppy will get the exercise he needs and rest when he's tired. Never force a puppy to exercise or encourage him to "overdo" it, as this puts stress on his growing frame.

Presas can suffer from elbow dysplasia as well as hip dysplasia. The breeders seeking to eradicate hip and elbow dysplasia from their lines must have their dogs x-rayed and exclude those affected dogs from their programs. Even if we take these measures, we know that some offspring will have a predisposition to hip dysplasia, but, generation after generation, we can actually reduce the number of dogs affected, and, as a result, the number of healthy dogs will continually increase.

Other orthopedic concerns for the Presa include panosteoitis (or "pano"), which causes the 5- to 12-month-old pup to limp on one leg or the other. It more frequently affects male puppies and may be linked to diet, another disease or heredity. Sometimes referred to as wandering lameness, the condition usually vanishes by the time the pup is two years of age and can be treated with anti-inflammatory medicine in the meantime.

OCD, or osteochondritis dessicans, is a condition that affects the young dog's cartilage and causes joint irritation, usually in the shoulder, elbow or ankle. It appears in dogs 4 to 18 months of age. Like pano, it is characterized by limping, though joint swelling and chronic pain often accompany the dog's limping. Rapid growth, excessive weight and strenuous exercise of the joints can aggravate this condition, which may warrant surgical intervention if other treatments fail. If not treated by a vet, your Presa can become lame.

More common in smaller breeds, patellar luxation (or slipped kneecap) have been cited in the Presa, the lateral form,

luxation, where the patella slips to the outside, being more common. Active adolescent dogs who exhibit problems moving or seem to have a knock-kneed stance exhibit the condition most often. Although not usually severe, surgical intervention may be called for in some cases, and the condition has been found in conjunction with anterior cruciate ligament tears, which have become more common in the Presa, usually caused by trauma to the knee joint. It can result in rear lameness.

The neurological disease known as Wobbler syndrome or cervical spondylolithesis affects Presas who are under one year of age, similar to the pattern seen in Great Danes. This is a hereditary condition that varies in severity. Badly affected animals are usually euthanized, though some dogs respond to the treatment and survive.

The Presa wants to be included in your daily routine. He needs companionship, love and attention, especially from his master. Do not consider this breed if you cannot make your Presa a top priority in your world.

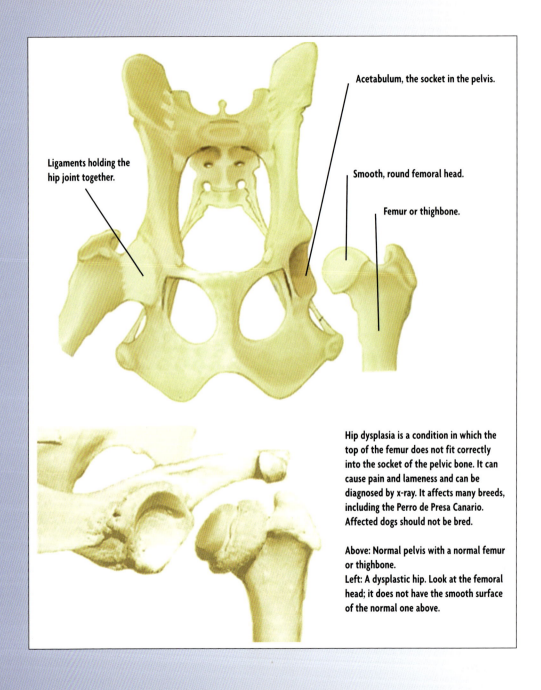

Acetabulum, the socket in the pelvis.

Ligaments holding the hip joint together.

Smooth, round femoral head.

Femur or thighbone.

Hip dysplasia is a condition in which the top of the femur does not fit correctly into the socket of the pelvic bone. It can cause pain and lameness and can be diagnosed by x-ray. It affects many breeds, including the Perro de Presa Canario. Affected dogs should not be bred.

Above: Normal pelvis with a normal femur or thighbone.
Left: A dysplastic hip. Look at the femoral head; it does not have the smooth surface of the normal one above.

Idiopathic epilepsy has been noted in the breed, a condition of unknown origins character-ized by seizures. Epilepsy is believed to have an inherited basis, so dogs that experience seizures should not be bred. Your vet can diagnose the condition and prescribe medica-tion to manage the seizures.

Breeders are also concerned about entropion, which is the rolling inward of the dog's eyes (usually both). Although more commonly seen in breeds like the Shar-pei or Chow Chow, it has been cited in the Presa. Severe cases can cause ulcera-tion, and surgery (eye tacking) is fairly successful, though it renders the dog ineligible to compete in dog shows.

Hypothyroidism, a common disorder in many purebred dogs, involves the insufficient activity of the thyroid gland. In the Canario, behavioral abnormali-ties, such as aggression or obsessive licking, may be symptoms of hypothyroidism, as are weight gain and loss or thinning of the haircoat. This condition is usually not life-threatening and can be managed with regular medication.

Psychological imbalance is another serious problem affecting Presas. Shyness, insecu-rity and irritability are usually associated with the condition, and the Presa is not exempted

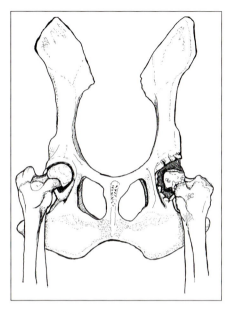

The healthy hip joint on the left and the unhealthy hip joint on the right.

from these problems, which are undesirable in every breed. Presas suffering from psycholog-ical imbalance can be dangerous to humans. Therefore, it is a major responsibility of the breeder not to use these dogs with these genetic problems in reproduction. The breeder has to keep in mind that he is reproducing dogs for society, and that the best way to serve that society is by providing it with sound, healthy dogs. When money is the motive, this premise is forgotten, and the price humans have to pay later is too high; sometimes, it is death. *Mentally healthy dogs* guard, defend and even attack if circumstances warrant, but they never kill anyone.

BREED STANDARD FOR THE
PERRO DE PRESA CANARIO

FIRST "BLUEPRINT" OF THE PRESA STANDARD

In the late 1970s, the author set the first standard of the Perro de Presa Canario into words for an article published in *Doggy People* magazine. A breed standard is a description in words of what the ideal representative of a given breed should look like. This first standard was simple and was based on the descriptions of the Presa provided by old-timers who knew the dogs in the Canary Islands plus some specific dimensions—size and weight—based on the author's first Presa (a dog named Boby). Boby, bred by Don Manuel Alemán, of Arucas, was a typical dog for that period, of moderate height and weight, with a light-brindle coat and a superb temperament.

The Spanish breed club, el Club Español del Presa Canario, was founded in 1982. In 1989, the Spanish Royal Canine Society accepted the standard for the Presa Canario. Solid-black dogs were not included in the first standard though they were included later that same year, when the first registration for the breed was held at the Canaries' Fair Institution, in Las Palmas, Grand Canary, on April 28, 1989.

The standard was clearly indispensable. Without it, it was practically impossible to "picture" the new Presa, which had been

MEETING THE IDEAL

The American Kennel Club defines a standard as: "A description of the ideal dog of each recognized breed, to serve as an ideal against which dogs are judged at shows." This "blueprint" is drawn up by the breed's recognized parent club, approved by a majority of its membership, and then submitted to the AKC for approval. The AKC states that "An understanding of any breed must begin with its standard. This applies to all dogs, not just those intended for showing." The picture that the standard draws of the dog's type, gait, temperament and structure is the guiding image used by breeders as they plan their programs. Although the AKC neither recognizes nor has a standard for the Presa Canario, the foregoing is a good explanation of the purpose of a breed standard.

bred since 1975. The standard was to become to guide for breeders. In most cases, a breed standard illustrates an imaginary dog, because the "perfect dog" that the standard describes does not exist in Nature. Mother Nature does not allow perfection in a living creature; thus, breeders attempt to produce a dog that is as close to perfection as possible. In the case of the new Presa, the standard indeed was used to recreate the breed, not just reproduce better typical specimens from existing typical specimens. That a breed standard is but a written document and, by its very nature, subject to interpretation by each person—breeder, judge, trainer, owner—who reads it, complicates the matter greatly. Thus, each breeder's interpretation, good, bad or indifferent, is in his mind's eye when he is selecting dogs for his own breeding program.

Worse yet, and this is a frequent and regrettable scenario, many Presa breeders today disregard the standard entirely when planning a breeding. The result is that the puppies produced, and the whole of a breeder's line, lack type and genetic consistency. Thus, today there are many different types of Presas around the world: some of which mirror the breed standard quite accurately, and others that bear no resemblance whatsoever,

in appearance or behavior, to the Presa described in the breed standard. Over the past quarter century, many breeders have continued to breed their Presas to other breeds that are imported into their countries. This only

BREEDER'S BLUEPRINT

If you are considering breeding your Presa Canario, it is very important that you are familiar with the breed standard. *Reputable breeders* breed with the intention of producing dogs that are as close as possible to the standard and that contribute to the advancement of the breed. Study the standard for both physical appearance and temperament, and make certain your bitch and your chosen stud dog measure up.

yields Presas that do not look like Presas and do not act like Presas, and thus are not Presas at all!

In time, the author believes that type will be firmly set in the breed, as has happened with other breeds. As the Spanish poet Antonio Machado says, *"Caminante no hay camino, se hace camino al andar."* (This is, roughly: "You who walk where there is no path, you make your path as you walk.") By breeding and selecting according to the standard, we are shaping the Perro de Presa Canario. Yet, a breed is not a breed until it is "officially recognized" by a national kennel club. In the Canary Islands and Spain, this is the Spanish Royal Canine Society (RSCE); throughout Europe and beyond, it is the Fédération Internationale Cynologique (FCI), which accepted the breed in June 2001 as the Dogo Canario, a name which the author and many others oppose. In the United Kingdom, the registry is known as The Kennel Club, which will likely never accept the Presa due to the country's "Dangerous Dog" laws. In the USA, where the Presa Canario has a promising future, the American Kennel Club (AKC), the United Kennel Club (UKC) and the States Kennel Club (SKC) are all-breed registries. The breed's parent club is the Dogo Canario Club of America.

BREED STANDARD FOR THE PERRO DE PRESA CANARIO
(Official Translation of the Breed Standard of the Club Español del Presa Canario)

Aspects considered by judges:

I. BREED NAME AND SYNONYM
Name: Presa Canario (in Spanish)
Synonym: Perro Basto and Verdino for brindled specimens.

II. ORIGINS AND DIFFUSION OF THE BREED
Molossoid dog, native to the islands of Tenerife and Gran Canaria, in the Canary Archipelago, where it was originally bred for fighting purposes. Basically the Presa dog is the result of crossbreeding between the Bardino or Majorero from the island of Fuerteventura and molossoid dogs that were introduced to the islands from abroad. Its fiery temperament is inherited from the Bardino, a prehispanic, hard-working and aggressive cattle dog, widely distributed throughout the islands. The resulting crossbreed has a black mask and a brindled or fawn coat with white spots. A few decades ago, a group of breeders began the process of recovering the breed, drawing on tradition and their experience. Since then, the Presa Canario has been carefully bred and widely promoted.

III. GENERAL APPEARANCE AND CHARACTER

1. Physical Description: Of medium height, eumetric, straight profile. Robust and well proportioned, mesomorphic, the body being longer than the height at the shoulder, more so in females. The head is large, square and wide-skulled. Slightly flaccid overlapping flews. Black mouth lining. Strong teeth, wide apart, generally fitting. Chestnut-colored eyes of medium size. Ears set high. Round, powerful, muscular neck with thick fur and loose skin. Slight dewlap. Short, straight back. Wide tail base. Chest wide and deep. Stomach slightly updrawn. Forequarters straight, wide-boned and strong cat feet. Powerful, muscular hindquarters with moderately angled stifles, with cat feet slightly longer than front feet. Thick, elastic skin. Short slightly rough hair without undercoat. Coat in brindled specimens should be fawn and black with black mask.

2. Character and Temperament: Powerful appearance, severe expression. Especially suited to protecting, guarding duties and traditionally used for herding cattle and dog-fighting. Impetuous temperament. Low, deep bark. Obedient, reliable family protector, unfriendly towards strangers.

BREEDING CONSIDERATIONS
The decision to breed your dog is one that must be considered carefully and researched thoroughly before moving into action. Some people believe that breeding will make their bitches happier or that it is an easy way to make money. Unfortunately, indiscriminate breeding only worsens the rampant problem of pet overpopulation, as well as putting a considerable dent in your pocketbook. As for the bitch, the entire process from mating through whelping is not an easy one and puts your pet under considerable stress. Last, but not least, consider whether or not you have the means to care for an entire litter of pups. Without a reputation in the field, your attempts to sell the pups may be unsuccessful.

Zygomatic arches very pronounced, with greatly developed jaw and cheek muscles. Marked depression between frontal lobes.

2.2. *Muzzle.* Shorter than the length of the skull, normally about 40% of the total head. Very wide. Straight or slightly convergent wrinkle.

2.3. *Lips or flews.* Fairly thick and fleshy. Upper flews not too pendulous, but forming an inverted "V" when viewed from the front. Inner lips may be pinkish but preferably dark.

2.4. *Jaws.* Teeth with very strong wide base, generally fitting. Slight prognatism (slightly undershot) acceptable, given the dog's origins. Bite typical of molossoid dogs. The absence of one or two premolars is not a fault, since the dog's function depends on its canines and incisors which should be well in line and well placed.

2.5. *Palate.* Well-marked pinkish grooves.

3. Eyes: Slightly oval. Well separated. Black eyelids. Color varies with coat from medium to very dark brown.

4. Ears: Hanging when complete. Medium sized, set high and wide apart. Generally rose. If, in

IV. Morphological Data

1. Height at shoulder: Males: 61 to 66 cms. (24 to 26 ins.). Females: 57 to 62 cms. (22.5 to 24.5 ins.).

2. Head: Brachycephalic type. Cubic tendency. Large and solid. Skull to face ratio 6:4. Furrow not accentuated.

2.1. *Skull.* Convex in anteposterior and transversal direction.

accordance with tradition, they are cut, they stand erect or semi-erect and are triangular in shape. Full eared dogs compete on equal terms with others.

5. Neck: Round, straight, solid and highly muscled. Shortish between 18 and 20 cms. (7–8 ins.). Loose skin below the throat forms a medium ridge.

6. Forequarters: Perfectly straight, well boned, set well apart, powerful musculature. Elbows turned neither in nor out. Compact cat-like feet. Strong nails, either black or light according to the coat.

7. Body: Longer than the height at the shoulder by about 20%. Wide chest, deep brisket level with elbows, with marked pectoral muscles. Thoracic perimeter at least 30% greater than shoulder height. Well-arched rib cage, almost cylindrical.

7.1. *Dorso-lumbar line* (from withers to loin). Straight, ascending slightly to the loins. Slight saddle effect just after the withers.

7.2. *Loin*. Straight, medium length and wide. Normally 1.5 cms. (.6 ins.) higher than the withers.

7.3. *Flanks*. Unpronounced.

8. Tail: Set on high, flexible, strong at the root and tapering to the hocks. At rest there may be lateral deviation. In action, elevated saber-like with the tip pointing forward but not curled.

9. Hindquarters: Hindlegs powerful, straight when viewed from the side or front. Very muscular second thighs, unpronounced angles. Cat-like feet. No spur normally. Hocks low and neither sickle nor cow. The presence of a spur is a fault but does not merit disqualification.

10. Coat:

10.1. *Hair*. Short all over, generally denser at withers, throat and top of loins. No underhair. Compact tail hair. Rough-looking, coarse.

Spanish Champion Urco, a veteran competing at the age of nine years old.

10.2. *Colour.* All types of brindle, from very warm dark colors to gray or very light brown or blonde. Full range of fawn to sand-colored. Occasionally there are markings around the neck or legs, where white marking is least desirable. In general, there are more or less long white markings on the chest. The mask is always dark and may extend around the eyes.

11. Weight: Average male: 45–57 kgs. (100–125 lbs.). Average female: 40–50 kgs. (88–110 lbs.).

12. Defects:

12.1. *Slight defects.*
• Excessive wrinkling of craneo-facial region.
• Presence of spur.

The gait, or movement, of the dog is assessed by the judge when the dog is competing.

12.2. *Serious defects.*
• Poor nose pigmentation.
• Excessive prognatism.
• Specimens with slight hound-like appearance.

• Poor mask.
• Sickle legged or cow hocks.
• Unbalanced character.
• Frail or thinnish appearance.
• Craneo-facial disproportion.
• Curled tail, of equal thickness all the way, amputated or mutilated.

12.3. *Total disqualification.*
• Monorchid, cryptorchid or castrated specimens.
• More than 20% white markings.
• Totally unpigmented nose or mouth lining.

Most important aspects:

1. Head (typicality): Massive. Muzzle well filled out. Dark colored eyes, well separated. Stop defined, but not too abrupt. Straight nose, not arched. Upper lip not withdrawn. Sufficient wrinkle. Well aligned bite, but not level. Reject specimens with level bite.

2. Body: Rectangular, longish, medium sized. Reject height that is neither functional nor characteristic. Well-sloped shoulders. Very arching ribs. Chest deep and the wider the better. Very well-developed pectorals. Separate elbows, not turned out. Strong-boned. Loins higher than withers, well developed. Slight angulation of hindlegs.

The Presa's head should be massive, with dark eyes and a straight nose. The ears can be cropped or natural, depending upon the rules of the given club or registry.

PERRO DE PRESA CANARIO

"YOU BETTER SHOP AROUND!"

Finding a reputable breeder who sells healthy pups is very important, but make sure that the breeder you choose is not only someone whom you respect but also someone with whom you feel comfortable. Your breeder will be a resource long after you buy your puppy, and you must be able to call with reasonable questions without being made to feel like a pest! If you don't connect on a personal level, investigate some other breeders before making a final decision.

CHOOSING A PRESA PUPPY

Many people go to see a breeder to get a puppy and tell the breeder that they want the "pick of the litter." "The pick of the litter?" I ask, perplexed. What do they mean by the best puppy of the litter? The strongest, the bravest, the most handsome, the most…? Or even the biggest?

Presas are not produced with a "cookie cutter"; they cannot all be identical—big, brave and strong! Even if this were possible, which it is not, the Presa is born and then raised. No matter how many good traits the puppy has inherited, without proper training and rearing, the Presa could still develop into a second-rate, or even unbalanced, dog.

I would say that the best Presa is the one who adjusts to the needs of the people with whom he lives. Of course, some temperaments are better suited to certain living arrangements than others. For example, a very active and dominant dog is not ideal for life in an apartment, where he will have to spend most of his time in a relatively small area. To live with a family, the most suitable

Presa is one of medium size who is emotionally balanced, not particularly dominant, yet extroverted and affectionate.

The most dominant and bravest dogs occasionally do not adjust well to living in apartments or condos because they need space to "get away" from the bosses—their owners. Constant nagging can make such a dog lose heart. The dominant Presa is, needless to say, the most suited for protection work. Everyone does not need a dog like this. You must consider if such a dog is suited to your needs and lifestyle.

When choosing a Presa, you should not consider the pup that cries noisily when you pick it up. This puppy is not a good choice for any pet owner, nor should it be used in a breeding program.

TESTING A PRESA PUPPY

As a responsible dog trainer and breeder of Presas, I am indebted to the "Campbell Test," devised by

Playtime with friends is more than just fun, it's an important part of a puppy's socialization, which is vital in developing a well-adjusted dog. This young Presa has plenty of friends to play with and learn from.

American psychologist William Campbell. This internationally regarded test on canine behavior is both practical and simple, proving to be of great help for breeders when selecting puppies from a litter. Likewise, I recognize the work of my friend, the late Polo Acosta y Acosta.

In the long, endless afternoons of coffee and chatting, mostly related to Presas, my dear friend Polo Acosta, always accompanied by his wife, used to say, "Crazy dogs are of no use, do you understand? Not for the family, nor for guarding, nor for driving or watching over the cattle, nor for

INHERIT THE MIND

In order to know whether or not a puppy will fit into your lifestyle, you need to assess his personality. A good way to do this is to interact with his parents. Your pup inherits not only his appearance but also his personality and temperament from the sire and dam. If the parents are fearful or overly aggressive, these same traits may show up in your puppy.

PUPPY PERSONALITY

When a litter becomes available to you, choosing a pup out of all those adorable faces will not be an easy task! Sound temperament is of utmost importance, but each pup has its own personality and some may be better suited to you than others. A feisty, independent pup will do well in a home with older children and adults, while quiet, shy puppies will thrive in a home with minimal noise and distractions. Your breeder knows the pups best and should be able to guide you in the right direction.

fighting nor for anything. The dog has to be like a human being: intelligent, observant, vigilant. It should never bite because dogs that bite can be dangerous, believe me. You should never use crazy or biting dogs for breeding because their descendants will be like them. Do use smart, brave and protective dogs.

"I once had a very smart dog, Marruecos. He knew how to

behave. He would never bark if there was no reason for barking and he was also a great guardian. Believe me, he never bothered anyone, and there was no other like him for fighting. These are the kinds of Presa that should be bred. Those nervous Presas that bark non-stop, whether they are tied or not, those that bite for no reason and those that do not respond to their master's commands are useless, one and all. You can tell that from the time they are puppies."

Due to Polo's physical limitations (he lost both legs from

PET INSURANCE

Just like you can insure your car, your house and your own health, you likewise can insure your dog's health. Investigate a pet insurance policy by talking to your vet. Depending on the age of your dog, the breed and the kind of coverage you desire, your policy can be very affordable. Most policies cover accidental injuries, poisoning and thousands of medical problems and illnesses, including cancers. Some carriers also offer routine care and immunization coverage, including heartworm preventative, prescription flea control, annual checkups, teeth cleaning, spaying/neutering, health screening and more. These policies are more costly than the others, but may be well worth the investment.

ARE YOU A FIT OWNER?
If the breeder from whom you are buying a puppy asks you a lot of personal questions, do not be insulted. Such a breeder wants to be sure that you will be a fit provider for his puppy.

gangrene), the author took him on many occasions to see the Presas, because this was what he always loved to do. One day, while we were having coffee, Polo Acosta told me that he wanted to visit my kennel to see my new litter of puppies. So we did, and Polo observed the litter: "Leave them there, let them go freely at their own pace, let them play and run. Puppies have to be carefully observed." Polo eyed two pups of the five, as if coming back from the past, and said, "Those two puppies could turn into

HANDLE WITH CARE
You should be extremely careful about handling tiny puppies. Not that you might hurt them, but that the pups' mother may exhibit what is called "maternal aggression." It is a natural, instinctive reaction for the dam to protect her young against anything she interprets as predatory or possibly harmful to her pups. The sweetest, most gentle of bitches, after whelping a litter, often reacts this way, even to her owner.

something important; of course, they still have to be raised, which is something that not everyone can do, as you know. Some people get a good puppy and they ruin it later on, because they don't know how to raise it even if they think they do. Pass me the brindle one; let's see if it goes through the test."

I took the puppy in my hands and gave it to him. Polo immediately grabbed it by the tail and swung it in the air from one side

Select a puppy that is affectionate and confident. Never settle for a puppy that is easily spooked, shy or otherwise unstable.

ARE YOU PREPARED?

Unfortunately, when a puppy is bought by someone who does not take into consideration the time and attention that dog ownership requires, it is the puppy who suffers when he is either abandoned or placed in a shelter by a frustrated owner. So all of the "homework" you do in preparation for your pup's arrival will benefit you both. The more informed you are, the more you will know what to expect and the better equipped you will be to handle the ups and downs of raising a puppy. Hopefully, everyone in the household is willing to do his part in raising and caring for the pup. The anticipation of owning a dog often brings a lot of promises from excited family members: "I will walk him every day," "I will feed him," "I will house-train him," etc., but these things take time and effort, and promises can easily be forgotten once the novelty of the new pet has worn off.

to the other as if to see if the puppy were made of rubber. Then he grabbed it by one ear and then by the other, and, quickly after that, he threw it to the floor without further ado. The puppy immediately stood up on his four legs, his tail up, as if nothing had happened, and went to join his brothers to play.

"Didn't I tell you?" said Don Polo, "That is a real dog. Don't you ever doubt it. Now hand me the fawn one." The fawn puppy responded just like his brother to Polo's test. The other three puppies did not, which pleased Polo. "They are weaker," he said, laughing, "You can sell them or do whatever you wish with them, but keep those two for yourself and you will tell me when they grow up."

After that, I showed Polo two three-month-old Majorero cattle puppies. One was a gray-sand-coated male called Major II and the other a brindle-coated bitch called Bardina. They were both born from Major I and Colilla. They both went through the test without complaint. "I have

A HEALTHY PUP

You should not even think about buying a puppy that looks sick, undernourished, overly frightened or nervous. Sometimes a timid puppy will warm up to you after a 30-minute "let's-get-acquainted" session.

TEMPERAMENT COUNTS

Your selection of a good puppy can be determined by your needs. A show potential or a good pet? It is your choice. Every puppy, however, should be of good temperament. Although show-quality puppies are bred and raised with emphasis on physical conformation, responsible breeders strive for equally good temperament. Do not buy from a breeder who concentrates solely on physical beauty at the expense of personality.

always liked cattle dogs," said Polo. "They are brave and resilient dogs. They are like no other and can be used for any purpose."

When I said good-bye to Don Polo, outside his house, in the road to Boquerón, he said to me, "Always test puppies the way I have showed you. You will see that it works, and beware of insecure, shy or crazy dogs." I pass the advice of this old-time Presa man on to breeders everywhere. It is fair to say that a buyer should not approach a litter and subject the puppy to Polo's test without the breeder's understanding and agreeing to the process.

Bring the children to meet the litter when you go to pick out your family dog. Socializing the pups with children is critical to the Presa's education. Presas naturally accept children and puppies especially love the attention of little humans.

PREPARING PUPPY'S PLACE IN YOUR HOME

Once you have researched the breed, found a good breeder, observed a litter or two and selected your puppy, you still will have some work to do before bringing home your chosen Presa puppy. You will have to prepare your home and family for the new addition. Much as you would prepare a nursery for a

YOUR SCHEDULE . . .

If you lead an erratic, unpredictable life, with daily or weekly changes in your work requirements, consider the problems of owning a puppy. The new puppy has to be fed regularly, socialized (loved, petted, handled, introduced to other people) and, most importantly, allowed to go outdoors for house-training. As the dog gets older, it can be more tolerant of deviations in its feeding and relief schedule.

PUPPY APPEARANCE

Your puppy should have a well-fed appearance but not a distended abdomen, which may indicate worms or incorrect feeding, or both. The body should be firm, with a solid feel. The skin of the abdomen should be pale pink and clean, without signs of scratching or rash. Check the hind legs to see if the dewclaws have been removed, if any were present at birth.

newborn baby, you will need to designate a place in your home that will be the puppy's own. You may prepare an outdoor kennel run for the dog as well. How you prepare your home indoors will depend on how much freedom the dog will be allowed. Whatever you decide, you must ensure that he has a place that he can "call his own."

When you bring your new puppy into your home, you are bringing him into what will become his home as well. Obviously, you did not buy a puppy with the intentions of catering to his every whim and allowing him to "rule the roost," but in order for a puppy to grow into a stable, well-adjusted dog, he has to feel comfortable in his surroundings. Remember, he is leaving the warmth and security of his mother and littermates, as well as the familiarity of the only place he has ever known, so it is important to make his transition as easy as possible. By preparing a place in your home for the puppy, you are making him feel as welcome as possible in a strange new place. It should not take him long to get used to it, but the sudden shock of being transplanted is somewhat traumatic for a young pup. Imagine how a small child would feel in the same situation—that is how your puppy must be feeling. It is up to you to reassure him and to let him know, "Little *perro*, you are going to like it here!"

WHAT YOU SHOULD BUY

CRATE
To someone unfamiliar with the use of crates in dog training, it may seem like punishment to shut a dog in a crate, but this is not the case at all. Although all

TIME TO GO HOME
Breeders rarely release puppies until they are eight to ten weeks of age. This is an acceptable age for most breeds of dog, excepting toy breeds, which are not released until around 12 weeks, given their petite sizes. If a breeder has a puppy that is 12 weeks of age or older, it is likely well social- ized and house-trained. Be sure that it is otherwise sound and healthy before deciding to take it home.

BOY OR GIRL?
An important consideration to be discussed is the sex of your puppy. For a family companion, a bitch may be the better choice, considering the female's inbred concern for all young creatures and her accompanying tolerance and patience. It is always advisable to spay a pet bitch, which may guarantee her a longer life.

breeders do not advocate crate training, more and more breeders and trainers are recommending crates as preferred tools for show puppies as well as pet puppies. Crates are not cruel—crates have many humane and highly effective uses in dog care and training. For example, crate training is a popular and very successful house-training method.

The Presa grows quickly and only the largest crate will do; purchase a crate for your puppy that will accommodate him at full size.

PHOTO COURTESY OF DOSKOCIL.

confined at night when they should be guarding their homes. With soft bedding and his favorite toy, a crate becomes a cozy pseudo-den for your dog. Like his ancestors, he too will seek out the comfort and retreat of a den.

As far as purchasing a crate, the type that you buy is up to you. It will most likely be one of the two most popular types: wire or fiberglass. There are advantages and disadvantages to each type. For example, a wire crate is more open, allowing the air to flow through and affording the dog a view of what is going on around him, while a fiberglass crate is sturdier. Both can double as travel crates, providing protection for the dog. The size of the crate is another thing to consider. Puppies do not stay puppies forever—in fact, sometimes it seems as if they grow right before your eyes. A small crate may be fine for a very young Presa pup, but it will not do him much good for long! Thus, it is better to get a crate that will accommodate your dog both as a pup and at full size. A large-size crate will be necessary for a full-grown Presa, who can stand up to 25 ins. (65 cms.) high.

In addition, a crate can keep your dog safe during travel and, perhaps most importantly, a crate provides your dog with a place of his own in your home. It serves as a "doggie bedroom" of sorts— your Presa can curl up in his crate when he wants to sleep or when he just needs a break. Many pups sleep in their crates overnight, though, once fully house-trained, they shouldn't be

BEDDING

Soft bedding or a crate pad in the dog's crate will help the dog feel more at home, and you may also like to give him a small blanket.

First, this will take the place of the leaves, twigs, etc., that the pup would use in the wild to make a den; the pup can make his own "burrow" in the crate. Although your pup is far removed from his den-making ancestors, the denning instinct is still a part of his genetic makeup. Second, until you take your pup home, he has been sleeping amid the warmth of his mother and litter-mates, and while a blanket is not the same as a warm, breathing body, it still provides heat and something with which to snuggle. You will want to wash your pup's bedding frequently in case he has a potty "accident" in his crate, and replace or remove any blanket or bedding that becomes ragged and starts to fall apart.

Toys

Toys are a must for dogs of all ages, especially for curious playful pups. Puppies are the "children" of the dog world, and what child does not love toys? Chew toys provide enjoyment for both dog and owner—your dog will enjoy playing with his favorite toys, while you will enjoy the fact that they distract him from chewing on your expensive shoes and leather sofa. Puppies love to chew; in fact, chewing is a physical need for pups as they are teething, and everything looks appetizing! The full range of your possessions—from old dish towel to Oriental carpet—are fair game in the eyes of a teething pup. Puppies are not all that discerning when it comes to finding something literally to "sink their teeth into"—everything tastes great!

Presa puppies are aggressive chewers and only the hardest, strongest toys should be offered to them. Breeders advise owners to resist stuffed toys, because they can become de-stuffed in no time. The overly excited pup may ingest the stuffing, which is neither nutritious nor digestible.

Similarly, squeaky toys are quite popular, but must be avoided for the Presa. Perhaps a squeaky toy can be used as an aid in training, but not for free play. If a pup "disembowels" one of

these, the small plastic squeaker inside can be dangerous if swallowed.

MENTAL AND DENTAL
Toys not only help your Presa Canario get the physical and mental stimulation he needs but also provide a great way to keep his teeth clean. Hard rubber or nylon toys, especially those constructed with grooves, are designed to scrape away plaque, preventing bad breath and gum infection.

TOYS, TOYS, TOYS!

With a big variety of dog toys available, and so many that look like they would be a lot of fun for a dog, be careful in your selection. It is amazing what a set of puppy teeth can do to an innocent-looking toy; so, obviously, safety is a major consideration. Be sure to choose the most durable products that you can find. Hard nylon bones and toys are a safe bet, and many of them are offered in different scents and flavors that will be sure to capture your dog's attention. It is always fun to play a game of fetch with your dog, and there are balls and flying discs that are specially made to withstand dog teeth.

Monitor the condition of all your pup's toys carefully and get rid of any that have been chewed to the point of becoming potentially dangerous.

Be careful of natural bones, which have a tendency to splinter into sharp, dangerous pieces. Also be careful of rawhide, which can turn into pieces that are easy to swallow and become a mushy mess on your carpet.

Lead

A nylon lead is probably the best option, as it is the most resistant to puppy teeth should your pup take a liking to chewing on his lead. Of course, this is a habit that should be nipped in the bud, but, if your pup likes to chew on his lead, he has a very slim chance of being able to chew through the strong nylon. Nylon leads are also lightweight, which is good for a young Presa who is just getting used to the idea of walking on a lead. For everyday walking and safety purposes, the nylon lead is a good choice. Being a strong dog, the adult Presa will require an equally strong lead, such as thick nylon or leather.

Collar

Your pup should get used to wearing a collar all the time since you will want to attach his ID tags to it; plus, you have to attach the leash to something! A lightweight nylon collar is a good choice. Make certain that the collar fits snugly enough so that the pup cannot wriggle out of it, but is loose enough so that it will not be uncomfortably tight around the pup's neck. You should be able to fit a finger between the pup's neck and the collar. It may take some time for your pup to get used to wearing the collar, but soon he will not even notice that it is there. The choke collar is made for training, but should only be used by an owner who has been instructed in its proper use.

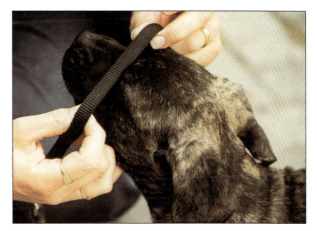

An adjustable nylon collar is the best choice to introduce the Presa puppy to wearing a collar. Always check it daily to make sure it is not too snug. Presa puppies grow hourly!

FOOD AND WATER BOWLS

Your pup will need two bowls, one for food and one for water. You may want two sets of bowls, one for indoors and one for outdoors, depending on where the dog will be fed and where he will be spending time. Stainless steel or sturdy plastic bowls are popular choices. Plastic bowls are more chewable, but dogs tend not to chew on the steel variety, which can be sterilized. It is important to buy sturdy bowls since anything is in danger of being chewed by puppy teeth and you do not want your dog to be constantly chewing apart his bowl (for his safety and for your purse!).

Many breeders recommend that Presa owners purchase bowl stands on which to elevate their

The Presa grows into a "big-boy" collar in no time. It is vital that your Presa's collar (and ID tags) are never missing. This owner has fashioned a small padlock to the collar to insure that it cannot be removed.

PHOTO COURTESY OF MIKKI PET PRODUCTS.

Your local pet shop will have an array of dishes and bowls, as well as bowl stands, suitable for your Perro de Presa Canario.

dogs' feeding bowls. This helps to ward off bloat, which can be caused by the dog's swallowing air, causing his stomach to twist. The results of bloat can be fatal, so any possible preventative should be welcomed advice.

CLEANING SUPPLIES

Until a pup is house-trained, you will be doing a lot of cleaning. "Accidents" will occur, which is acceptable in the beginning stages of toilet training because the puppy does not know any better. All you can do is be prepared to clean up any accidents as soon as they happen. Old rags, towels, newspapers and a safe disinfectant are good to have on hand.

BEYOND THE BASICS

The items previously discussed are the bare necessities. You will find out what else you need as you go along—grooming supplies, flea/tick protection, baby gates to partition a room, etc. These things will vary depending on your situation, but it is important that you have everything you need to feed and make your Presa comfortable in his first few days at home.

PUPPY-PROOFING YOUR HOME

Aside from making sure that your Presa will be comfortable in your home, you also have to make sure that your home is safe for your Presa. This means taking precau-

PLAY'S THE THING

Teaching the puppy to play with his toys in running and fetching games is an ideal way to help the puppy develop muscle, learn motor skills and bond with you, his owner and master. He also needs to learn how to inhibit his bite reflex and never to use his teeth on people, forbidden objects and other animals in play. Whenever you play with your puppy, you make the rules. This becomes an important message to your puppy in teaching him that you are the pack leader and control everything he does in life. Once your dog accepts you as his leader, your relationship with him will be cemented for life.

tions that your pup will not get into anything he should not get into and that there is nothing within his reach that may harm him should he sniff it, chew it, inspect it, etc. This probably seems obvious since, while you are primarily concerned with your pup's safety, at the same time you do not want your belongings to be ruined. Breakables should be placed out of reach if your dog is to have full run of the house. If he is to be limited to certain places within the house, keep any potentially dangerous items in the "off-limits" areas.

An electrical cord can pose a danger should the puppy decide to taste it—and who is going to

convince a pup that it would not make a great chew toy? Cords should be kept from puppy teeth and fastened tightly against the wall. If your pup is going to spend time in a crate, make sure that there is nothing near his crate that he can reach if he sticks his

NATURAL TOXINS

Examine your lawn and home landscaping before bringing your puppy home. Many varieties of plants have leaves, stems or flowers that are toxic if ingested, and you can depend on a curious puppy to investigate them. Ask your vet for information on poisonous plants or research them at your library.

curious little nose or paws through the openings. Just as you would with a child, keep all household cleaners and chemicals where the pup cannot reach them.

It is also important to make sure that the outside of your

TOXIC PLANTS

Many plants can be toxic to dogs. If you see your dog carrying a piece of vegetation in his mouth, approach him in a quiet, disinterested manner, avoid eye contact, pet him and gradually remove the plant from his mouth. Alternatively, offer him a treat and maybe he'll drop the plant on his own accord. Be sure no toxic plants are growing in your own garden.

SKULL & CROSSBONES

Thoroughly puppy-proof your house before bringing your puppy home. Never use cockroach or rodent poisons or plant fertilizers in any area accessible to the puppy. Avoid the use of toilet cleaners. Most dogs are born with "toilet-bowl sonar" and will take a drink if the lid is left open. Also keep the trash secured and out of reach.

home is safe. Of course, your puppy should never be unsuper-vised, but a pup let loose in the yard will want to run and explore, and he should be granted that freedom. Do not let a fence give you a false sense of security; you would be surprised at how crafty (and persistent) a dog can be in working out how to dig under and squeeze his way through small holes, or to jump or climb over a fence. The remedy is to make the fence well embedded into the ground and high enough so that it really is impossible for your dog to get over it (about 6 feet should suffice). Be sure to repair or secure any gaps in the fence. Check the fence periodically to ensure that it is in good shape and make repairs as needed; a very determined pup may return to the same spot to "work on it" until he is able to get through.

HOW VACCINES WORK

If you've just bought a puppy, you surely know the importance of having your pup vaccinated, but do you understand how vaccines work? Vaccines contain the same bacteria or viruses that cause the disease you want to prevent, but they have been chemically modified so that they don't cause any harm. Instead, the vaccine causes your dog to produce antibodies that fight the harmful bacteria. Thus, if your pup is exposed to the disease in the future, the antibodies will destroy the viruses or bacteria.

FIRST TRIP TO THE VET

You have selected your puppy, and your home and family are ready. Now all you have to do is collect your Presa from the breeder and the fun begins, right? Well...not so fast. Something else you need to plan is your pup's first trip to the vet. Perhaps the breeder can recommend someone in the area who specializes in mastiff or other large breeds, or maybe you know some other responsible dog owners who can suggest a good vet. Either way, you should have an appointment arranged for your pup before you pick him up.

The pup's first visit will consist of an overall examination to make sure that the pup does not have any problems that are not apparent to you. The vet will also set up a schedule for the pup's vaccinations; the breeder will inform you of which ones the pup has already received and the vet can continue from there.

INTRODUCTION TO THE FAMILY

Everyone in the house will be excited about the puppy's coming home and will want to pet him and play with him, but it is best to make the introduction low-key so as not to overwhelm the puppy. He is apprehensive already. It is the first time he has been separated from his mother and the breeder, and the ride to your home is likely to be the first time he has been in a car. The last thing you want to do is smother him, as this will only frighten him further. This is not to say that human contact is not extremely necessary at this stage,

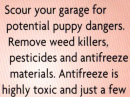

CHEMICAL TOXINS

Scour your garage for potential puppy dangers. Remove weed killers, pesticides and antifreeze materials. Antifreeze is highly toxic and just a few drops can kill a puppy or an adult dog. The sweet taste attracts the animal, who will quickly consume it from the floor or pavement.

because this is the time when a connection between the pup and his human family is formed. Gentle petting and soothing words should help console him, as well as just putting him down and letting him explore on his own (under your watchful eye, of course).

The pup may approach the family members or may busy himself with exploring for a while. Gradually, each person should spend some time with the pup, one at a time, crouching down to get as close to the pup's level as possible, letting him sniff their hands and petting him gently. He definitely needs human attention and he needs to be touched—this is how to form an immediate bond. Just remember that the pup is experiencing many things for the first time, at the same time. There are new people, new noises, new smells and new things to investigate, so be gentle, be affectionate and be as comforting as you can be.

PUP'S FIRST NIGHT HOME
You have traveled home with your new charge safely in his crate. He's been to the vet for a thorough check-up; he's been weighed, his papers have been examined and perhaps he's even been vaccinated and wormed as well. He's met the whole family, including the excited children and the less-than-happy cat. He's explored his area, his new bed, the yard and anywhere else he's been permitted. He's eaten his first meal at home and relieved himself in the proper place. He's heard lots of new sounds, smelled new friends and seen more of the outside world than ever before... and that was just the first day! He's worn out and is ready for bed...or so you think!

It's puppy's first night home and you are ready to say "Good night." Keep in mind that this is his first night ever to be sleeping alone. His dam and littermates are no longer at paw's length and he's a bit scared, cold and lonely. Be reassuring to your new family member, but this is not the time to spoil him and give in to his inevitable whining.

Puppies whine. They whine to let others know where they are and hopefully to get company out of it. Place your pup in his new bed or crate in his designated area and close the crate door. Mercifully, he may fall asleep without a peep. When the inevitable occurs, however, ignore the whining—he is fine. Be strong and keep his interest in mind. Do not allow yourself to feel guilty and visit the pup. He will fall asleep eventually.

Many breeders recommend placing a piece of bedding from the pup's former home in his new bed so that he recognizes and is comforted by the scent of his

littermates. Others still advise placing a hot water bottle in the bed for warmth. The latter may be a good idea provided the pup doesn't attempt to suckle—he'll get good and wet, and may not fall asleep so fast.

Puppy's first night can be somewhat stressful for both the pup and his new family. Remember that you are setting the tone of nighttime at your house. Unless you want to play with your pup every night at 10 p.m., midnight and 2 a.m., don't initiate the habit. Your family will thank you, and so will your pup!

IN DUE TIME

It will take at least two weeks for your puppy to become accustomed to his new surroundings. Give him lots of love, attention, handling, frequent opportunities to relieve himself, a diet he likes to eat and a place he can call his own.

Presa puppies are tolerant of being handled by children, though adult supervision is warranted whenever children are playing with a puppy or adult dog.

PREVENTING PUPPY PROBLEMS

SOCIALIZATION

Now that you have done all of the preparatory work and have helped your pup get accustomed to his new home and family, it is about time for you to have some fun! Socializing your Presa pup gives you the opportunity to show off your new friend, and your pup gets to reap the benefits of being a fascinating creature that people will want to pet and, in general, think is truly exceptional!

Besides getting to know his new family, your puppy should be exposed to other people, animals and situations. This will help him become well adjusted as he grows up and less prone to being timid or fearful of the new things he will encounter. Of course, he must not come into close contact with dogs you don't know well until his course of injections is fully complete.

Your pup's socialization began with the breeder, but now it is your responsibility to continue it. The socialization he receives until the age of 12 weeks is the most critical, as this is the time when he forms his impressions of the outside world. Be especially careful during the eight-to-ten-week-old period, also known as the fear period. The interaction he receives during this time should be gentle and reassuring. Lack of

socialization, and/or negative experiences during the socialization period, can manifest itself in fear and aggression as the dog grows up. Your puppy needs lots of positive interaction, which of course includes human contact, affection, handling and exposure to other animals.

Once your pup has received his necessary vaccinations, feel free to take him out and about (on his lead, of course). Walk him around the neighborhood, take him on your daily errands, let people pet him, let him meet other dogs and pets, etc. Puppies do not have to try to make friends; there will be no shortage of people who will want to introduce themselves. Just make sure that you carefully supervise each meeting. If the neighborhood children want to say hello, for example, that is great—children and pups most often make great

---

PROPER SOCIALIZATION

Thorough socialization includes not only meeting new people but also being introduced to new experiences such as riding in the car, having his coat brushed, hearing the television, walking in a crowd—the list is endless. The more your pup experiences, and the more positive the experiences are, the less of a shock and the less frightening it will be for your pup to encounter new things.

SOCIALIZATION PERIOD

The socialization period for puppies is from age 8 to 16 weeks. This is the time when puppies need to leave their birth family and take up residence with their new owners, where they will meet many new people, other pets, etc. Failure to be adequately socialized can cause the dog to grow up fearing others and being shy and unfriendly due to a lack of self-confidence.

companions. However, sometimes an excited child can unintentionally handle a pup too roughly, or an overzealous pup can playfully nip a little too hard.

You want to make socialization experiences positive ones. What a pup learns during this very formative stage will affect his attitude toward future encounters. You want your dog to be comfortable around everyone. A pup that has a bad experience with a child may grow up to be a dog that is shy around or aggressive toward children.

CONSISTENCY IN TRAINING

Dogs, being pack animals, naturally need a leader, or else they try to establish dominance in their packs. When you welcome a dog into your family, the choice of who becomes the leader and who becomes the "pack" is entirely up to you! Your pup's intuitive quest

for dominance, coupled with the fact that it is nearly impossible to refuse a Presa pup, give the pup almost an unfair advantage in getting the upper hand! A pup will definitely test the waters to see what he can and cannot do. Do not give in to those pleading eyes—stand your ground when it

MANNERS MATTER

During the socialization process, a puppy should meet people, experience different environments and definitely be exposed to other canines. Through playing and interacting with other dogs, your puppy will learn lessons, ranging from controlling the pressure of his jaws by biting his littermates to the inner-workings of the canine pack that he will apply to his human relationships for the rest of his life. That is why removing a puppy from his litter too early (before eight weeks) can be detrimental to the pup's development.

Your Presa puppy will look to you to become his leader. A dog as potentially powerful as the Presa requires a strong, confident master. Impress upon your Presa puppy that you are his ideal pack leader.

comes to disciplining the pup and make sure that all family members do the same. It will only confuse the pup if Mother tells him to get off the sofa when he is used to sitting up there with Father to watch the nightly news. Avoid discrepancies by having all members of the household decide on the rules before the pup even comes home...and be consistent

in enforcing them! Early training shapes the dog's personality, so you cannot be unclear in what you expect.

COMMON PUPPY PROBLEMS
The best way to prevent puppy problems is to be proactive in stopping an undesirable behavior as soon as it starts. The old saying "You can't teach an old dog new

PUPPY PROBLEMS

The majority of problems that are commonly seen in young pups will disappear as your dog gets older. However, how you deal with problems when he is young will determine how he reacts to discipline as an adult dog. It is important to establish who is boss (hopefully it will be you!) right away when you are first bonding with your dog. This bond will set the tone for the rest of your life together.

tricks" does not necessarily hold true, but it is true that it is much easier to discourage bad behavior in a young developing pup than to wait until the pup's bad behavior becomes the adult dog's bad habit. There are some problems that are especially prevalent in puppies as they develop.

NIPPING

As puppies start to teethe, they feel the need to sink their teeth into anything available...unfortunately, that usually includes your fingers, arms, hair and toes. You may find this behavior cute for

GOING PRO

Training your puppy takes much patience and can be frustrating at times, but you should see results from your efforts. If you have a puppy that seems untrainable, take him to a trainer or behaviorist. The dog may have a personality problem that requires the help of a professional, or perhaps you need help in learning how to train your dog.

the first five seconds...until you feel just how sharp those puppy teeth are. Nipping is something you want to discourage immediately and consistently with a firm "No!" (or whatever number of firm "Nos" it takes for him to understand that you mean business). Then, replace your finger with an appropriate chew toy. While this behavior is merely annoying when the dog is young, it can become dangerous as your Presa's adult teeth grow in and his jaws develop, and he continues to think it is okay to gnaw on human appendages. Your Presa does not mean any harm with a friendly nip, but he also does not know his own strength.

CRYING/WHINING

Your pup will often cry, whine, whimper, howl or make some type of commotion when he is left alone. This is basically his way of calling out for attention to make sure that you know he is there and that you have not forgotten about him. Your puppy feels insecure when he is left

CHEWING TIPS

Chewing goes hand in hand with nipping in the sense that a teething puppy is always looking for a way to soothe his aching gums. In this case, instead of chewing on you, he may have taken a liking to your favorite shoe or something else which he should not be chewing. Again, realize that this is a normal canine behavior that does not need to be discouraged, only redirected. Your pup just needs to be taught what is acceptable to chew on and what is off-limits. Consistently tell him "No!" when you catch him chewing on something forbidden and give him a chew toy. Conversely, praise him when you catch him chewing on something appropriate. In this way you are discouraging the inappropriate behavior and reinforcing the desired behavior. The puppy's chewing should stop after his adult teeth have come in, but an adult dog continues to chew for various reasons—perhaps because he is bored, needs to relieve tension or just likes to chew. That is why it is important to redirect his chewing when he is still young.

alone, when you are out of the house and he is in his crate or when you are in another part of the house and he cannot see you. The noise he is making is an expression of the anxiety he feels at being alone, so he needs to be taught that being alone is okay. You are not actually training the dog to stop making noise; rather, you are training him to feel comfortable when he is alone and thus removing the need for him to make the noise.

This is where the crate with cozy bedding and a toy comes in handy. You want to know that your pup is safe when you are not there to supervise, and you know that he will be safe in his crate rather than roaming freely about the house. In order for the pup to stay in his crate without making a fuss, he first needs to be comfort-

CRATE-TRAINING TIPS

During crate training, you should partition off the section of the crate in which the pup stays. If he is given too big an area, this will hinder your training efforts. Crate training is based on the fact that a dog does not like to soil his sleeping quarters, so it is ineffective to keep a pup in a crate that is so big that he can eliminate in one end and get far enough away from it to sleep. Also, you want to make the crate den-like for the pup. Blankets and a favorite toy will make the crate cozy for the small pup; as he grows, you may want to evict some of his "roommates" to make more room. It will take some coaxing at first, but be patient. Given some time to get used to it, your pup will adapt to his new home-within-a-home quite nicely.

able in his crate. On that note, it is extremely important that the crate is never used as a form of punishment; this will cause the pup to view the crate as a negative place, rather than as a place of his own for safety and retreat.

Accustom the pup to the crate in short, gradually increasing time intervals in which you put him in the crate, maybe with a treat, and stay in the room with him. If he cries or makes a fuss, do not go to him, but stay in his sight. Gradually he will realize that staying in his crate is okay without your help, and it will not be so traumatic for him when you are not around. You may want to leave the radio on softly when you leave the house; the sound of human voices may be comforting to him.

Crate training pays off dividends throughout the dog's life, not only in puppyhood but also in adulthood. Crates are the ideal means to transport a dog to and from the vet, dog shows, family outings and more.

DIETARY AND FEEDING CONSIDERATIONS

Today the choices of food for your Presa are many and varied. There are simply dozens of brands of food in all sorts of flavors and textures, ranging from puppy diets to those for seniors. There are even hypoallergenic and low-calorie diets available. Because your Presa's food has a bearing on coat, health and temperament, it is essential that the most suitable diet is selected for a Presa of his age. It is fair to say, however, that even experienced owners can be perplexed by the enormous range of foods available. Only understanding what is best for your dog will help you reach an informed decision.

Dog foods are produced in three basic types: dry, semi-moist and canned. Dry foods are useful for the cost-conscious, for overall they tend to be less expensive than semi-moist or canned foods. Dry foods also contain the least fat and the most preservatives. In general, canned foods are made up of 60–70% water, while semi-moist ones often contain so much sugar that they are perhaps the least preferred by owners, even though their dogs seem to like them.

A diet of solely dry food, while wholeheartedly recom-

STORING DOG FOOD
You must store your dry dog food carefully. Open packages of dog food quickly lose their vitamin value, usually within 90 days of being opened. Mold spores and vermin could also contaminate the food.

mended by many experts, is disputed by others, including the author, who believes that Presas should be offered more variety, like the diet of a wolf on the hunt seeking a variety of foods (from deer and elk to greens and berries). Add raw meat to the Presa's ration of dry food, as the dog's system is able to digest raw meat, as it would in the wild. Owners should include some raw meat on occasion for both puppies and adults.

Doubtless to say, a dog's health is directly related to what he eats and the activities he performs. It is true that many urban dogs are obese, just like their owners, and that is beneficial neither to the dogs nor to their owners. The best solution to help an obese dog lose weight is to engage in some daily exercise, not simply to reduce the food portion, which may help too.

When selecting your dog's diet, three stages of development must be considered: the puppy stage, the adult stage and the senior or veteran stage.

PUPPY STAGE

Puppies instinctively want to suck milk from their mother's teats; a normal puppy will exhibit this behavior just a few moments following birth. If puppies do not attempt to suckle within the first half-hour or so, they should be encouraged to do so by placing

FOOD PREFERENCE

Selecting the best dry dog food is difficult. There is no majority consensus among veterinary scientists as to the value of nutrient analyses (protein, fat, fiber, moisture, ash, cholesterol, minerals, etc.). All agree that feeding trials are what matter most, but you also have to consider the individual dog. The dog's weight, age and activity level, and what pleases his taste, all must be considered. It is probably best to take the advice of your vet or breeder. Every dog's dietary requirements vary, even during the lifetime of a particular dog.

Opinions differ about whether it is best to feed the Presa commercial food, fresh food or a combination of both. Seek the advice of the breeder of your dog to find out about which feeding practices he has had success. Keep in mind that commercial food is usually balanced, and adding extras can offset the balance.

them on the nipples, having selected ones with plenty of milk. This early milk supply is important in providing the essential colostrum, which protects the puppies during the first eight to ten weeks of their lives. Although a mother's milk is much better than any milk formula, despite there being some excellent ones available, if the puppies do not feed, the breeder will have to feed them by hand. For those with less experience, advice from a vet is important so that not only the right quantity of milk is fed but also that of correct quality, fed at suitably frequent intervals, usually every two hours during the first few days of life.

GRAIN-BASED DIETS

Some less expensive dog foods are based on grains and other plant proteins. While these products may appear to be attractively priced, many breeders prefer a diet based on animal proteins and believe that they are more conducive to your dog's health. Many grain-based diets rely on soy protein, which may cause flatulence (passing gas).

There are many cases, however, when your dog might require a special diet. These special requirements should only be recommended by your vet.

The breeder introduces the puppies to solid foods before they leave for new homes. It is advisable to resume feeding the same type of food that the breeder recommends.

Puppies should be allowed to nurse from their mothers for about the first six weeks, although, starting around the third or fourth week, the breeder will begin to introduce small portions of suitable solid food. Most breeders like to introduce alternate milk and meat meals initially, building up to weaning time.

By the time the puppies are

Be prepared when it's time to feed your Presa!

THE CANINE GOURMET

Your dog does not prefer a fresh bone. Indeed, he wants it properly aged and, if given such a treat indoors, he is more likely to try to bury it in the carpet than he is to settle in for a good chew! If you have a yard, give him such delicacies outside and guide him to a place suitable for his "bone yard." He will carefully place the treasure in its earthy vault and seemingly forget about it. His seeming distaste or lack of thanks for your thoughtfulness is not that at all. He will return in a few days to inspect the bone, perhaps to re-bury it, and when it is just right, he will relish it as much as you do that cooked-to-perfection steak. If he is in a concrete or bricked kennel run, he will be especially frustrated at the hopelessness of the situation. He will vacillate between ignoring it completely, giving it a few licks to speed the curing process with saliva, and trying to hide it behind the water bowl! When the bone has aged a bit, he will set to work on it.

seven or a maximum of eight weeks old, they should be fully weaned and fed solely on a proprietary puppy food. Selection of the most suitable, good-quality diet at this time is essential, for a puppy's fastest growth rate is during the first year of life. Vets are usually able to offer advice in this regard and, although the frequency of meals will be reduced over time, only when a young dog has reached the age of about 12 months should an adult diet be fed. Puppy and junior diets should be well balanced for the needs of your dog so that, except in certain circumstances, additional vitamins, minerals and proteins will not be required.

FEEDING TIPS

Dog food must be at room temperature, neither too hot nor too cold. Fresh water, changed often and served in a clean bowl, is mandatory, especially when feeding dry food.

Never feed your dog from the table while you are eating, and never feed your dog leftovers from your own meal. They usually contain too much fat and too much seasoning.

Dogs must chew their food. Hard pellets are excellent; soups and stews are to be avoided. Chewing hard food keeps the jaws in shape and helps to keep the teeth clean.

Except for age-related changes, dogs do not require dietary variations, though they appreciate variety just as humans do.

ADULT DIETS

A dog is considered an adult when it has stopped growing, so in general the diet of a Presa can be changed to an adult one at about 12 months of age although the dog may take more time to fully mnature physically. Again you should rely upon your vet or dietary specialist to recommend an acceptable maintenance diet, whether you choose to feed commercial food or a diet you create at home. It is necessary for you to select the type of diet best suited to your dog's needs. Active dogs have different requirements than sedate dogs.

SENIOR DIETS

As dogs get older, their metabolism changes. The older dog usually exercises less, moves more slowly and sleeps more. This change in lifestyle and physiological performance requires a change in diet. Since these changes take place slowly, they might not be recognizable. What is easily recognizable is weight gain. By continuing to feed your dog an adult-maintenance diet when it is slowing down metabolically, your dog will gain weight. Obesity in an older dog compounds the health problems that already accompany old age.

As your dog gets older, few of its organs function up to par. The kidneys slow down and the intestines become less efficient.

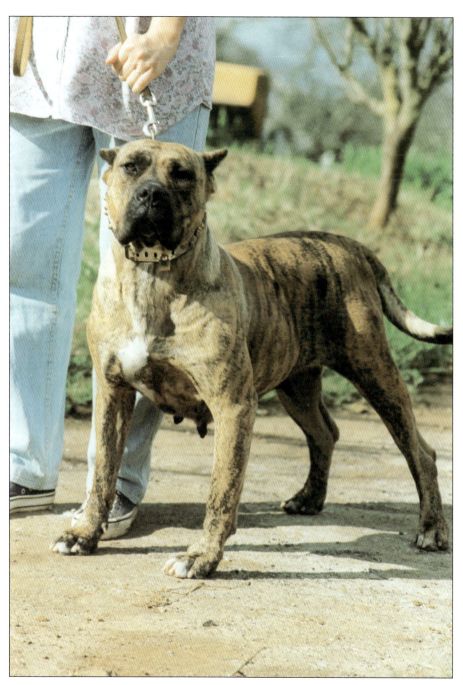

Feeding requirements vary from dog to dog, but you want your Presa to look as vibrant as this bitch does and feeding plays a vital part in your Presa's good health and overall appearance.

DRINK, DRANK, DRUNK— MAKE IT A DOUBLE

In both humans and dogs, as well as other living organisms, water forms the major part of nearly every body tissue. Naturally, we take water for granted, but without it, life as we know it would cease.

For dogs, water is needed to keep their bodies functioning biochemically. Additionally, water is needed to replace the water lost while panting. Unlike humans, who are able to sweat to dissipate heat, dogs must pant to cool down, thereby losing the vital water that their bodies need to regulate their body temperatures. Humans lose electrolyte-containing products and other body-fluid components through sweating; dogs do not lose anything except water.

Water is essential always, but especially so when the weather is hot or humid or when your dog is exercising or working vigorously.

DO DOGS HAVE TASTE BUDS?

Watching a dog "wolf" or gobble his food, seemingly without chewing, leads an owner to wonder whether his dog can taste anything. Yes, dogs have taste buds, with sensory perception of sweet, salty and sour. Puppies are born with fully mature taste buds.

These age-related factors are best handled with a change in diet and a change in feeding schedule to give smaller portions that are more easily digested. There is no single best diet for every older dog. While many dogs do well on light or senior diets, other dogs do better on puppy diets or other special premium diets such as lamb and rice. Be sensitive to your senior Presa's diet, as this will help control other problems that may arise with your old friend.

WATER

Just as your dog needs proper nutrition from his food, water is an essential "nutrient" as well. Water keeps the dog's body properly hydrated and promotes normal function of the body's systems. During house-training, it is necessary to keep an eye on how much water your Presa is drinking, but once he is reliably trained he should have access to clean fresh water at all times, especially if you feed dry food. Make certain that the dog's water

OBESITY AND BOREDOM

Bear in mind that an overweight dog should never be suddenly over-exercised; instead he should be encouraged to increase exercise slowly. Not only is exercise essential to keep the dog's body fit, it is essential to his mental well-being. A bored dog will find something to do, which often manifests itself in some type of destructive behavior. In this sense, exercise is essential for the owner's mental well-being as well!

bowl is clean, and change the water often.

EXERCISE

Exercise is important to the Presa, though the dog does not need to run in wide open spaces all day long. The Presa does not thrive if confined to a small area, such as a small yard. If your home only has limited accommodations for the Presa, then you must take your dog out daily to the park or any enclosed, safe area where the dog can run and play. Be sure that dogs are permitted in any public place that you choose to bring your Presa.

Because of the possibility of bloat, an owner should take care not to exercise the Presa within at least an hour before and after feeding. Likewise, in order to minimize the risk of hip dysplasia, young puppies should not be exercised strenuously while their

TIPPING THE SCALES

Good nutrition is vital to your dog's health, but many people end up over-feeding or giving unnecessary supplements. Here are some common doggie diet don'ts:
- Adding milk, yogurt and cheese to your dog's diet may seem like a good idea for coat and skin care, but dairy products are very fattening and can cause indigestion.
- Diets high in fat will not cause heart attacks in dogs but will certainly cause your dog to gain weight.
- Most importantly, don't assume your dog will simply stop eating once he doesn't need any more food. Given the chance, he will eat you out of house and home!

bones are still forming and growing.

There are many ways to provide the Presa with exercise; the best are those that give owner and dog interaction and time to spend together. Play is very important to the Presa, and the owner should involve himself in games with his dog. In a pack, wolves, very social animals like their relatives, dogs, are constantly playing games.

It is useful to realize that the canine is a gregarious creature and prefers to live among other dogs. Dogs prefer their own species to any other, including humans, though some silly owners choose to think otherwise. If circumstances permit, the author recommends you to acquire a male and a bitch. Do not get two same-sex animals, as quarrels will occur and sometimes these can have dire even grave outcomes. No matter how we try, we can never replace the company of another dog, but, nevertheless, we should return to the discussion of fun and games with your Presa.

"DOES THIS COLLAR MAKE ME LOOK FAT?"
While humans may obsess about how they look and how trim their bodies are, many people believe that extra weight on their dogs is a good thing. The truth is, pets should not be over- or under-weight, as both can lead to or signal sickness. In order to tell how fit your pet is, run your hands over his ribs. Are his ribs buried under a layer of fat or are they sticking out considerably? If your pet is within his normal weight range, you should be able to feel the ribs easily, but they should not protrude abnormally. If you stand above him, the outline of his body should resemble an hourglass. Some breeds do tend to be leaner while some are a bit stockier, but making sure your dog is the right weight for his breed will certainly contribute to his good health.

The most important thing in your relationship with your Presa is how you treat him every day in your home and yard. Games are absolutely essential to your dog's emotional balance. Dogs con-

LET SLEEPING PRESAS LIE!
Dogs consume more oxygen than humans, which is one reason that owners shouldn't sleep in the same room with their dogs. Least of all should a dog sleep in his owner's bed with the windows and door closed. It is much safer for dogs to sleep in their own room, in their own crates or beds. If you live in a temperate climate, your Presa can sleep outside the house or in his own kennel area. Of course, in inclement or cold/hot weather, the Presa should sleep indoors.

stantly play among themselves, so it's your goal to engage the Presa in enjoyable activities, such as chasing a ball or flying disk or the like. Dogs use play to establish their emotional ties to and relationships among members of the pack. You are a member of the Presa's pack—ideally the leader. Without hierarchy, dogs cannot function nor relate to one another. By your actions, being the one to initiate and carry out the "play," your dog will come to know that you are the Alpha dog (or bitch). Dogs are natural observers and understand their place in the family (pack).

In caring for your Presa, establishing and enjoying a good relationship with your dog is as important as providing proper food, exercise and veterinary care. The rapport that you establish with your Perro de Presa Canario should provide constant benefits to both parties.

GROOMING

BRUSHING
Since the Presa is a short-coated breed, very little grooming is required. A natural bristle brush or a hound glove can be used for regular routine brushing. Regular brushing is effective for removing dead hair and stimulating the dog's natural oils to add shine and a healthy look to the coat. Even though the Presa's coat is short

Your local pet shop sells an assortment of grooming tools from which you may choose those tools necessary to keep your Presa's coat clean and healthy.

Puppies learn cleanliness from adult dogs. For such an active breed of working dog, the Presa requires very little in the way of grooming and bathing.

and close, it does require a five-minute once-over every few days to keep it looking its shiny best. Regular grooming sessions are also a good way to spend time with your Presa. Many dogs grow to like the feel of being brushed and will come to enjoy the routine.

BATHING

Dogs do not need to be bathed as often as humans, but regular bathing is essential for healthy skin and a healthy, shiny coat. Presas do not need to be bathed more than a few times per year, unless they get particularly dirty or roll in something smelly. Again, like most anything, if you accustom your pup to being bathed as a puppy, it will be

SOAP IT UP

The use of human soap products like shampoo, bubble bath and hand soap can be damaging to a dog's coat and skin. Human products are too strong; they remove the protective oils coating the dog's hair and skin that make him water-resistant. Use only shampoo made especially for dogs. You may like to use a medicated shampoo, which will help to keep external parasites at bay.

BATHING BEAUTY

Once you are sure that the dog is thoroughly rinsed, absorb the excess water out of his coat by drying him with a heavy towel. You may choose to use a blow dryer on low heat on his coat or just let it dry naturally. In cold weather, never allow your dog outside with a wet coat.

There are "dry bath" products on the market, which are sprays and powders intended for spot cleaning, that can be used between regular baths if necessary. They are not substitutes for regular baths, but they are easy to use for touch-ups as they do not require rinsing.

second nature by the time he grows up. You want your dog to be at ease in the bathtub or else it could end up a wet, soapy, messy ordeal for both of you!

Give your Presa a once-over with the brush or glove before wetting his coat. This will get rid of any debris and dead hair, which are harder to remove when the coat is wet. Make certain that your dog has a good non-slip surface on which to stand. Begin by wetting the dog's coat, checking the water temperature to make sure that it is neither too hot nor too cold. A shower or hose attachment is necessary for thoroughly wetting and rinsing the coat.

Next, apply shampoo to the dog's coat and work it into a good lather. Wash the head last, as you do not want shampoo to drip into the dog's eyes while you are washing the rest of his body. You

Nail Maintenance

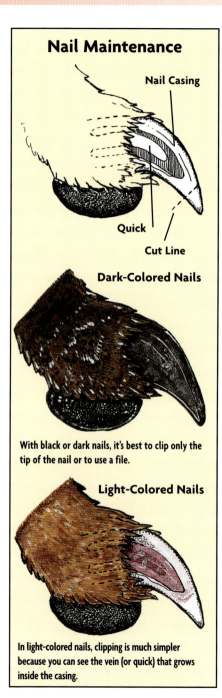

Nail Casing

Quick

Cut Line

Dark-Colored Nails

With black or dark nails, it's best to clip only the tip of the nail or to use a file.

Light-Colored Nails

In light-colored nails, clipping is much simpler because you can see the vein (or quick) that grows inside the casing.

NAIL FILING

You can purchase an electric tool to grind down a dog's nails rather than cut them. Some dogs don't seem to mind the electric grinder but will object strongly to nail clippers. Talking it over with your vet will help you make the right choice.

should use only a shampoo that is made for dogs. Do not use a product made for human hair. Work the shampoo all the way down to the skin. You can use this opportunity to check the skin for any bumps, bites or other abnormalities. Do not neglect any area of the body—get all of the hard-to-reach places.

Once the dog has been thoroughly shampooed, he requires an equally thorough rinsing. Shampoo left in the coat can be irritating to the dog's skin. Protect his eyes from the shampoo by shielding them with your hand and directing the flow of water in the opposite direction. You should also avoid getting water in the ear canal. Be prepared for your dog to shake out his coat— you might want to stand back, but make sure you have a hold on the dog to keep him from running through the house.

EAR CLEANING

The ears should be kept clean with a cotton wipe and ear powder or liquid made especially for dogs. Do not probe into the ear canal with a cotton swab, as this can cause injury. Be on the lookout for any signs of infection or ear-mite infestation. If your Presa has been shaking his head or scratching at his ears frequently, this usually indicates a problem. If the dog's ears have an unusual odor, this is a sure sign of mite infestation or infection, and a signal to have his ears checked by the vet.

NAIL CLIPPING
Your Presa should be accustomed to having his nails trimmed at an early age, since nail clipping will be part of your maintenance routine throughout his life. Not only does it look nicer, but long nails can scratch someone

PEDICURE TIP
A dog that spends a lot of time outside on a hard surface, such as cement or pavement, will have his nails naturally worn down and may not need to have them trimmed as often, except maybe in the colder months when he is not outside as much. Regardless, it is best to get your dog accustomed to the nail-trimming procedure at an early age so that he is used to it. Some dogs are especially sensitive about having their feet touched, but if a dog has experienced it since puppyhood, it should not bother him.

unintentionally. Also, a long nail has a better chance of ripping and bleeding, or causing the feet to spread. A good rule of thumb is that if you can hear your dog's nails' clicking on the floor when he walks, his nails are too long.

Before you start cutting, make sure you can identify the "quick" in each nail. The quick is a blood vessel that runs through the center of each nail and grows rather close to the end. The quick will bleed if accidentally cut, which will be quite painful for the dog as it contains nerve endings. Keep some type of clotting agent on hand, such as a styptic pencil or styptic powder (the type used for shaving). This will stop the bleeding quickly when applied to the end of the cut nail. Do not panic if you cut the quick, just stop the bleeding and talk soothingly to your dog. Once he has calmed down, move on to the next nail. It is better to clip a little at a time, particularly with black-nailed dogs.

Hold your pup steady as you begin trimming his nails; you do not want him to make any sudden movements or run away. Talk to him soothingly and stroke him as you clip. Holding his foot in your hand, simply take off the end of each nail with one swift clip. You should purchase nail clippers that are made for use on dogs; you can probably find them wherever you buy grooming supplies.

TRAVELING WITH YOUR DOG

CAR TRAVEL

You should accustom your Presa to riding in a car at an early age. You may or may not take him in the car often, but at the very least he will need to go to the vet and you do not want these trips to be traumatic for the dog or troublesome for you. The safest way for a dog to ride in the car is in his crate. If he uses a crate in the house, you can use the same crate for travel, provided you have a vehicle large enough to accommodate the crate.

Put the pup in the crate and see how he reacts. If he seems uneasy, you can have a passenger hold him on his lap while you drive. Another option for car travel is a specially made safety harness for dogs, which straps the dog in much like a seat belt. If you have a sport utility or similar vehicle, you can partition the back section, effectively creating a "crate" within the vehicle. Whichever option you choose, do not let the dog roam loose in the vehicle—this is very dangerous! If you should stop short, your dog can be thrown and injured. If the dog starts climbing on you and pestering you while you are driving, you will not be able to concentrate on the road. It is an unsafe situation for everyone—human and canine.

For long trips, be prepared to stop to let the dog relieve himself. Take with you whatever you need to clean up after him, including some paper towels and some old bath towels for use should he have a potty accident in the car or suffer from motion sickness.

AIR TRAVEL

Every airline has different and specific rules and regulations regarding transporting dogs. You will have to follow the airline's guidelines regarding health certification, food, water, travel crates, etc. For example, the dog will be required to travel in an airline-approved crate, so you must check in advance with the airline regarding specific requirements.

To help put the dog at ease during travel, give him one of his favorite toys in the crate. Do not feed the dog for several hours before checking in, in order to minimize his need to relieve himself. However, regulations usually require you to attach a supply of food and two bowls for food and water to the outside of the crate so that airline employees can tend to the dog.

Make sure your dog is properly identified and that your contact information appears on his ID tags and on his crate. Animals travel in a different area of the plane than human passengers, so every rule must be strictly followed so as to prevent the risk of getting separated from your dog.

VACATIONS AND BOARDING

So you want to take a family vacation—and you want to include *all* members of the family. You would probably make arrangements for accommodations ahead of time anyway, but this is especially important when traveling with a dog. You do not want to make an overnight stop at the only place around for miles, only to find out that they do not allow dogs. Also, you do not want to reserve a place for your family without confirming that you are traveling with a dog, because, if it is against their policy, you may end up without a place to stay.

Alternatively, if you are traveling and choose not to bring your Presa, you will have to make arrangements for him while you are away. Some options are to take him to a neighbor's house to stay while you are gone, to have a trusted neighbor stop by often or stay at your house or to bring your dog to a reputable boarding kennel. Sometimes the dog's breeder will take care of him while you are away. If you choose to board him at a kennel, you should visit in advance to see the facilities provided and where the dogs are kept. Are the dogs' areas spacious and kept clean? Talk to some of the employees and see how they treat the dogs—have they experience with large, potentially aggressive breeds, do they spend time with the dogs, play with them, exercise

them, etc.? Be sure to introduce your Presa to the staff so that he accepts these strangers as friends. Also find out the kennel's policy on vaccinations and what they require. This is for all of the dogs' safety, since there is a greater risk of diseases being passed from dog to dog when dogs are kept together.

IDENTIFICATION

Your Presa is your valued companion and friend. That is why you always keep a close eye on him and you have made sure that he cannot escape from the yard or wriggle out of his collar and run away from you. However, accidents can happen and there may come a time when your dog unexpectedly becomes separated from you. If this unfortunate event should occur, the first thing on your mind will be finding him. Proper identification, including an ID tag, a tattoo and possibly a microchip, will increase the chances of his being returned to you safely and quickly.

TRAINING YOUR
PERRO DE PRESA CANARIO

Any dog is a big responsibility and, if not trained sensibly, may develop unacceptable behavior that annoys you or could even cause family friction. To train your Presa, you may like to enroll in an obedience class. Teach your dog good manners as you learn how and why he behaves the way he does. Find out how to communicate with your dog and how to recognize and understand his communications with you. Suddenly the dog takes on a new role in your life—he is clever, interesting, well behaved and fun to be with. He demonstrates his bond of devotion to you daily.

Those involved with teaching dog obedience and counseling owners about their dogs' behavior have discovered some interesting facts about dog ownership. For example, training dogs when they are puppies results in the highest rate of success in developing well-mannered and well-adjusted adult dogs. Training an older dog, from six months to six years of age, can produce almost equal results, providing that the owner accepts the dog's slower rate of learning capability and is willing to work

patiently to help the dog succeed at developing to his fullest potential. Unfortunately, many owners of untrained adult dogs lack the patience factor, so they do not persist until their dogs are successful at learning particular behaviors.

Training a puppy aged 10 to 16 weeks (20 weeks at the most) is like working with a dry sponge in a pool of water. The pup soaks up whatever you show him and constantly looks for more things to do and learn. At this early age, his body is not yet producing hormones, and therein lies the reason for such a high rate of success. Without hormones, he is focused on his owners and not particularly interested in investigating other places, dogs, people, etc. You are his leader: his provider of food, water, shelter and security. He latches onto you and wants to stay close. He will usually follow you from room to room, will not let you out of his sight when you are outdoors with him and will respond in like manner to the people and animals you encounter. If you greet a friend warmly, he will be happy to greet the person as well. If, however, you are hesitant or anxious about the approach of a stranger, he will respond accordingly.

Once the puppy begins to produce hormones, his natural curiosity emerges and he begins to investigate the world around him. It is at this time when you may notice that the untrained dog begins to wander away from you and even ignore your commands to stay close. When this behavior becomes a problem, you have two choices: get rid of the dog or train him. It is strongly urged that you choose the latter option.

For the Presa, formal obedience classes are recommended as structure and discipline are crucial to the dog's behavioral development. You usually will be able to find obedience classes within a reasonable distance from your home, but you can also do a lot to train your dog yourself. Sometimes there are classes available, but the tuition is too costly. Whatever the circumstances, the solution to training your dog without obedience classes lies within the pages of this book.

This chapter is devoted to helping you train your Presa Canario at home. If the recommended procedures are followed faithfully, you may expect positive results that will prove rewarding both to you and your dog.

PARENTAL GUIDANCE

Training a dog is a life experience. Many parents admit that much of what they know about raising children they learned from caring for their dogs. Dogs respond to love, fairness and guidance, just as children do. Become a good dog owner and you may become an even better parent.

Whether your new charge is a puppy or a mature adult, the methods of teaching and the techniques we use in training basic behaviors are the same. After all, no dog, whether puppy or adult, likes harsh or inhumane methods. All creatures, however, respond favorably to gentle motivational methods and sincere praise and encouragement. Now let us get started.

HOUSE-TRAINING

You can train a puppy to relieve himself wherever you choose, but this must be somewhere suitable. You should bear in mind from the outset that when your puppy is old enough to go out in public places, any canine deposits must be removed at once. You will always have to carry with you a plastic bag or "poop-scoop."

Outdoor training includes such surfaces as grass, soil and cement. Indoor training usually means training your dog to news-paper (which is not ideal for the Presa). When deciding on the surface and location that you will want your Presa to use, be sure it is going to be permanent. Training your dog to grass and then chang-ing your mind a few months later is extremely difficult for both dog and owner.

Next, choose the command you will use each and every time you want your puppy to void. "Hurry up" and "Let's potty" are examples of commands com-monly used by dog owners. Get in the habit of giving the puppy your chosen relief command before you take him out. That way, when he becomes an adult, you will be able to determine if he wants to go out when you ask him. A confirmation will be signs of interest such as wagging his tail, watching you intently, going to the door, etc.

PUPPY'S NEEDS

The puppy needs to relieve himself after play periods, after each meal, after he has been sleeping and at any time he indicates that he is looking for a place to urinate or defecate. The urinary and intestinal tract muscles of very young puppies are not fully developed. Therefore, like human babies, puppies need to relieve themselves frequently.

Take your puppy out often—every hour for an eight-week-old, for example—and always immedi-ately after sleeping and eating. The older the puppy, the less often he will need to relieve himself. Finally, as a mature healthy adult, he will require only three to five relief trips per day.

HOUSING

Since the types of housing and control you provide for your puppy have a direct relationship on the success of house-training, we consider the various aspects of both before we begin training.

TAKE THE LEAD

Do not carry your puppy to his relief area. Lead him there on a lead or, better yet, encourage him to follow you to the spot. If you start carrying him to his spot, you might end up doing this routine for longer than your back will permit and your dog will have the satisfaction of having trained *you*.

CANINE DEVELOPMENT SCHEDULE

It is important to understand how and at what age a puppy develops into adulthood. If you are a puppy owner, consult the following Canine Development Schedule to determine the stage of development your puppy is currently experiencing. This knowledge will help you as you work with the puppy in the weeks and months ahead.

Period	Age	Characteristics
FIRST TO THIRD	BIRTH TO SEVEN WEEKS	Puppy needs food, sleep and warmth, and responds to simple and gentle touching. Needs mother for security and disciplining. Needs littermates for learning and interacting with other dogs. Pup learns to function within a pack and learns pack order of dominance. Begin socializing with adults and children for short periods. Begins to become aware of its environment.
FOURTH	EIGHT TO TWELVE WEEKS	Brain is fully developed. Needs socializing with outside world. Remove from mother and littermates. Needs to change from canine pack to human pack. Human dominance necessary. Fear period occurs between 8 and 12 weeks. Avoid fright and pain.
FIFTH	THIRTEEN TO SIXTEEN WEEKS	Training and formal obedience should begin. Less association with other dogs, more with people, places, situations. Period will pass easily if you remember this is pup's change-to-adolescence time. Be firm and fair. Flight instinct prominent. Permissiveness and over-disciplining can do permanent damage. Praise for good behavior.
JUVENILE	FOUR TO EIGHT MONTHS	Another fear period about 7 to 8 months of age. It passes quickly, but be cautious of fright and pain. Sexual maturity reached. Dominant traits established. Dog should understand sit, down, come and stay by now.

NOTE: THESE ARE APPROXIMATE TIME FRAMES. ALLOW FOR INDIVIDUAL DIFFERENCES IN PUPPIES.

Taking a new puppy home and turning him loose in your house can be compared to turning a child loose in a sports arena and telling the child that the place is all his! The sheer enormity of the place would be too much for him to handle. Instead, offer the puppy clearly defined areas where he can play, sleep, eat and live. A room of the house where the family gathers is the most obvious choice. Puppies are social animals and need to feel a part of the pack right from the start. Hearing your voice, watching you while you are doing things and smelling you nearby are all positive reinforcers that he is now a member of your pack. Usually a family room, the kitchen or a nearby adjoining breakfast area is ideal for providing safety and security for both puppy and owner.

Within the designated room, there should be a smaller area that the puppy can call his own. An alcove, a wire or fiberglass dog crate or a fenced (not boarded!) corner from which he can view the activities of his new family will be fine. The size of the area or crate is the key factor here. The area must be large enough so that the puppy can lie down and stretch out, as well as stand up, without rubbing his head on the top. At the same time, it must be small enough so that he cannot relieve himself at one end and sleep at the other without coming

into contact with his droppings before he is fully trained to relieve himself outside. Dogs are, by nature, clean animals and will not remain close to their relief areas unless forced to do so. In those cases, they then become dirty dogs and usually remain that way for life.

The dog's designated area should contain clean bedding and a toy. Water can be put in his crate or area, in a non-spill container, once house-training has been achieved reliably.

CONTROL
By *control*, we mean helping the puppy to create a lifestyle pattern that will be compatible to that of his human pack (YOU!). Just as we guide little children to learn our way of life, we must show the

puppy when it is time to play, eat, sleep, exercise and even entertain himself.

Your puppy should always sleep in his crate. He should also learn that, during times of house-hold confusion and excessive human activity, such as at breakfast when family members are preparing for the day, he can play by himself in relative safety and comfort in his designated area. Each time you leave the puppy alone, he should under-stand exactly where he is to stay.

Puppies are chewers. They cannot tell the difference between lamp cords, television wires, shoes, table legs, etc. Chewing into a television wire, for example, can be fatal to the puppy while a shorted wire can start a fire in the house. If the puppy chews on the arm of the chair when he is alone, you will probably discipline him angrily when you get home. Thus, he makes the association that your coming home means he is going to be punished. (He will not remember chewing the chair and is incapable of making the associa-tion of the discipline with his naughty deed.) Accustoming the pup to his designated area not only keeps him safe but also avoids his engaging in destructive behaviors when you are not around.

Times of excitement, such as special occasions, family parties, etc., can be fun for the puppy, providing that he can view the activities from the security of his designated area. He is not underfoot and he is not being fed all sorts of tidbits that will probably cause him stomach distress, yet he still feels a part of the fun.

SCHEDULE

A puppy should be taken to his relief area each time he is released from his designated area, after meals, after play sessions and when he first awakens in the morning (at age eight weeks, this can mean 5 a.m.!). The puppy will indicate that he's ready "to go" by circling or sniffing busily—do not misinterpret these signs. For a puppy less than ten weeks of age, a routine of taking him out every

The male of the species makes more of an event out of every potty trip. This macho ritual can occur on any vertical object, so proper house-training early on pays off for the dog's whole life.

hour is necessary. As the puppy grows, he will be able to wait for longer periods of time.

Keep trips to his relief area short. Stay no more than five or six minutes and then return to the house. If he goes during that time, praise him lavishly and take him indoors immediately. If he does not, but he has an accident when you go back indoors, pick him up immediately, say "No! No!" and return to his relief area. Wait a few minutes, then return to the house again. Never hit a puppy or put his face in urine or excrement when he has had an accident!

Once indoors, put the puppy in his crate until you have had time to clean up his accident. Then, release him to the family area and watch him more closely than before. Chances are, his accident was a result of your not picking up his signal or waiting too long before offering him the

THE SUCCESS METHOD
6 Steps to Successful Crate Training

1 Tell the puppy "Crate time!" and place him in the crate with a small treat (a piece of cheese or half of a biscuit). Let him stay in the crate for five minutes while you are in the same room. Then release him and praise lavishly. Never release him when he is fussing. Wait until he is quiet before you let him out.

2 Repeat Step 1 several times a day.

3 The next day, place the puppy in the crate as before. Let him stay there for ten minutes. Do this several times.

4 Continue building time in five-minute increments until the puppy stays in his crate for 30 minutes with you in the room. Always take him to his relief area after prolonged periods in his crate.

5 Now go back to Step 1 and let the puppy stay in his crate for five minutes, this time while you are out of the room.

6 Once again, build crate time in five-minute increments with you out of the room. When the puppy will stay willingly in his crate (he may even fall asleep!) for 30 minutes with you out of the room, he will be ready to stay in it for several hours at a time.

THE SUCCESS METHOD

Success that comes by luck is usually short-lived. Success that comes by well-thought-out proven methods is often more easily achieved and permanent. This is the Success Method. It is designed to give you, the puppy owner, a simple yet proven way to help your puppy develop clean living habits and a feeling of security in his new environment.

Crate training provides safety for you, the puppy and the home. It also provides the puppy with a feeling of security, and that helps the puppy achieve self-confidence and clean habits. Remember that one of the primary ingredients in house-training your puppy is control. Regardless of your lifestyle, there will always be

opportunity to relieve himself. Never hold a grudge against the puppy for accidents.

Let the puppy learn that going outdoors means it is time to relieve himself, not to play. Once trained, he will be able to play indoors and out and still differentiate between the times for play versus the times for relief.

Help him develop regular hours for naps, being alone, playing by himself and just resting, all in his crate. Encourage him to entertain himself while you are busy with your activities. Let him learn that having you near is comforting, but it is not your main purpose in life to provide him with undivided attention.

Each time you put your puppy in his own area, use the same command, whatever suits best. Soon he will run to his crate or special area when he hears you say those words.

HOW MANY TIMES A DAY?

AGE	RELIEF TRIPS
To 14 weeks	10
14–22 weeks	8
22–32 weeks	6
Adulthood	4
(dog stops growing)	

These are estimates, of course, but they are a guide to the *minimum* number of opportunities a dog should have each day to relieve himself.

occasions when you will need to have a place where your dog can stay and be happy and safe. Crate training is the answer for now and in the future.

In conclusion, a few key elements are really all you need for a successful house-training method—consistency, frequency, praise, control and supervision. By following these procedures with a normal, healthy puppy, you and the puppy will soon be past the stage of "accidents" and ready to move on to a full and rewarding life together.

ROLES OF DISCIPLINE, REWARD AND PUNISHMENT

Discipline, training one to act in accordance with rules, brings order to life. It is as simple as that. Without discipline, particularly in a group society, chaos will reign supreme and the group will eventually perish. Humans and canines are social animals and need some form of discipline in order to function effectively. They must procure food, protect their home base and their young and reproduce to keep their species going. If there were no discipline in the lives of social animals, they would eventually die from starvation and/or predation by other stronger animals.

In the case of domestic canines, discipline in their lives is needed in order for them to understand how their pack (you and other family members) functions and how they must act in order to survive.

A large humane society in a highly populated area recently surveyed dog owners regarding their satisfaction with their relationships with their dogs. People who had trained their dogs were 75% more satisfied with their pets than those who had never trained their dogs.

Dr. Edward Thorndike, a noted psychologist, established *Thorndike's Theory of Learning*, which states that a behavior that results in a pleasant event tends to be repeated, and a behavior that results in an unpleasant event tends not to be repeated. It is this theory upon which many training methods are based today. For example, if you manipulate a dog to perform a specific behavior and reward him for doing it, he is likely to do it again because he enjoyed the end result.

Occasionally, punishment, a penalty inflicted for an offense, is necessary. The best type of punishment often comes from an outside source. For example, a child is told not to touch the stove because he may get burned. He disobeys and touches the stove. In doing so, he receives a burn. From that time on, he respects the heat of the stove and avoids contact with it. Therefore, a behavior that results in an unpleasant event tends not to be repeated.

Start crate training as soon as your new Presa puppy arrives at your home. Soon your puppy will regard his crate as a place all his own. Purchase a crate that will be large enough for the Presa once he's reached his adult size.

A good example of a dog learning the hard way is the dog who chases the house cat. He is told many times to leave the cat alone, yet he persists in teasing the cat. Then, one day, the dog begins chasing the cat but the cat turns and swipes a claw across the dog's face, leaving the dog with a painful gash on his nose. The final result is that the dog stops chasing the cat. Again, a behavior that results in an unpleasant event tends not to be repeated.

TRAINING EQUIPMENT

COLLAR AND LEAD
For a Presa pup, the collar and lead that you use for training must be one with which you are easily able to work, not too heavy for the dog and perfectly safe.

TREATS
Have a bag of treats on hand; something nutritious and easy to swallow works best. Use a soft treat, a chunk of cheese or a piece of cooked chicken rather than a dry biscuit. By the time the dog has finished chewing a dry treat, he will forget why he is being rewarded in the first place!

Using food treats will not teach a dog to beg at the table—the only way to teach a dog to beg at the table is to give him food from the table. In training, rewarding the dog with a food treat will help him associate praise and the treats with learning new behaviors that obviously please his owner.

TRAINING BEGINS: ASK THE DOG A QUESTION
In order to teach your dog anything, you must first get his attention. After all, he cannot learn anything if he is looking away from you with his mind on something else.

To get your dog's attention, ask him "School?" and immediately walk over to him and give him a treat as you tell him "Good dog." Wait a minute or two and repeat the routine, this time with a treat in your hand as you approach within a foot of the dog. Do not go directly to him, but stop about a foot short of him and hold out the treat as you ask "School?" He will see you approaching with a treat in your hand and most likely begin walking toward you. As you meet, give him the treat and praise again.

The third time, ask the question, have a treat in your hand and walk only a short distance toward the dog so that he must walk almost all the way to you. As he reaches you, give him the treat and praise again.

By this time, the dog will probably be getting the idea that if he pays attention to you, especially when you ask that question, it will pay off in treats

When training the Presa, be firm and consistent in doling out correction. Impressed by praise, Presas live to please their masters, so punishment is rarely necessary.

and enjoyable activities for him. In other words, he learns that "school" means doing great things with you that are fun and that result in positive attention for him.

Remember that the dog does not understand your verbal language; he only recognizes sounds. Your question translates to a series of sounds for him, and those sounds become the signal to go to you and pay attention. The dog learns that if he does this, he will get to interact with you plus receive treats and praise.

TEACHING THE BASIC COMMANDS

THE SIT EXERCISE
Now that you have the dog's attention, attach his lead and hold

it in your left hand, and hold a food treat in your right hand. Place your food hand at the dog's nose and let him lick the treat but not take it from you. Say "Sit"

If your Presa proves a bit more stubborn than you expect, a little pressure on his hindquarters will reinforce the goal of the sit command.

and slowly raise your food hand from in front of the dog's nose up over his head so that he is looking at the ceiling. As he bends his head upward, he will have to bend his knees to maintain his balance. As he bends his knees, he will assume a sit position. At that point, release the food treat and praise lavishly with com-

DOUBLE JEOPARDY

A dog in jeopardy never lies down. He stays alert on his feet because instinct tells him that he may have to run away or fight for his survival. Therefore, if a dog feels threatened or anxious, he will not lie down. Consequently, it is important to keep the dog calm and relaxed as he learns the down exercise.

ments such as "Good dog! Good sit!," etc. Remember to always praise enthusiastically, because dogs relish verbal praise from their owners and feel so proud of themselves whenever they accomplish a behavior.

You will not use food forever in getting the dog to obey your commands. Food is only used to teach new behaviors and, once the dog knows what you want when you give a specific command, you will wean him off the food treats but still maintain the verbal praise. After all, you will always have your voice with you, and there will be many times when you have no food rewards but expect the dog to obey.

THE DOWN EXERCISE

Teaching the down exercise is easy when you understand how the dog perceives the down position, and it is very difficult when you do not. Dogs perceive the down position as a submissive one; therefore, teaching the down exercise by using a forceful method can sometimes make the dog develop such a resentment of the down that he either runs away when you say "Down" or he attempts to snap at the person who tries to force him down.

Have the dog sit close alongside your left leg, facing in the same direction as you are. Hold the lead in your left hand and a food treat in your right.

Now place your left hand lightly on the top of the dog's shoulders where they meet above the spinal cord. Do not push down on the dog's shoulders; simply rest your left hand there so you can guide the dog to lie down close to your left leg rather than to swing away from your side when he drops.

Now place the food hand at the dog's nose, say "Down" very softly (almost a whisper) and slowly lower the food hand to the dog's front feet. When the food hand reaches the floor, begin moving it forward along the floor in front of the dog. Keep talking softly to the dog, saying things like, "Do you want this treat? You can do this, good dog." Your reassuring tone of voice will help calm the dog as he tries to follow the food hand in order to get the treat.

When the dog's elbows touch the floor, release the food and praise softly. Try to get the dog to maintain that down position for several seconds before you let him sit up again. The goal here is to get the dog to settle down and not feel threatened in the down position.

The stay command is the natural extension of the down (or sit) command. This puppy is being trained to down-stay with a hand signal.

THE STAY EXERCISE

It is easy to teach the dog to stay in either a sit or a down position. Again, we use food and praise during the teaching process as we help the dog to understand exactly what it is that we are expecting him to do.

To teach the sit/stay, start with the dog sitting on your left side as before and hold the lead in your left hand. Have a food treat in your right hand and place your food hand at the dog's nose. Say "Stay" and step out on your right foot to stand directly in front of the dog, toe to toe, as he licks and

CONSISTENCY PAYS OFF

Dogs need consistency in their feeding schedule, exercise and relief visits, and in the verbal commands you use. If you use "Stay" on Monday and "Stay here, please" on Tuesday, you will confuse your dog. Don't demand perfect behavior during training sessions and then let him have the run of the house the rest of the day. Above all, lavish praise on your pet consistently every time he does something right. The more he feels he is pleasing you, the more willing he will be to learn.

Once a Presa puppy is properly trained to walk and heel, even a child could lead him.

nibbles the treat. Be sure to keep his head facing upward to maintain the sit position. Count to five and then swing around to stand next to the dog again with him on your left. As soon as you get back to the original position, release the food and praise lavishly.

To teach the down/stay, do the down as previously described. As soon as the dog lies down, say "Stay" and step out on your right foot just as you did in the sit/stay. Count to five and then return to stand beside the dog with him on your left side. Release the treat and praise as always.

Within a week or ten days, you can begin to add a bit of distance between you and your dog when you leave him. When you do, use your left hand open with the palm facing the dog as a stay signal, much the same as the hand signal a police officer uses to stop traffic at an intersection.

Hold the food treat in your right hand as before, but this time the food will not be touching the dog's nose. He will watch the food hand and quickly learn that he is going to get that treat as soon as you return to his side.

When you can stand 1 yard away from your dog for 30 seconds, you can then begin building time and distance in both stays. Eventually, the dog can be expected to remain in the stay position for prolonged periods of time until you return to him or call him to you. Always praise lavishly when he stays.

THE COME EXERCISE

If you make teaching "come" an exciting experience, you should never have a student that does not love the game or that fails to come when called. The secret, it seems, is never to teach the word "come."

At times when an owner most wants his dog to come when

"WHERE ARE YOU?"

When calling the dog, do not say "Come." Say things like, "Pedro, where are you? See if you can find me! I have a biscuit for you!" Keep up a constant line of chatter with coaxing sounds and frequent questions such as "Where are you?" The dog will learn to follow the sound of your voice to locate you and receive his reward.

You can also teach your Presa to stay in the "stand" position. This is a necessity for show dogs, as the dogs must stand politely for evaluation by the judge.

called, the owner is likely to be upset or anxious and he allows these feelings to come through in the tone of his voice when he calls his dog. Hearing that desperation in his owner's voice, the dog fears the results of going to him and therefore either disobeys outright or runs in the opposite direction. The secret, therefore, is to teach the dog a game and, when you want him to come to you, simply play the game. It is practically a no-fail solution!

To begin, have several members of your family take a few food treats and each go into a different room in the house. Everyone takes turns calling the dog, and each person should celebrate the dog's finding him with a treat and lots of happy praise. When a person calls the dog, he is actually inviting the dog to find him and to get a treat as a reward for "winning."

A few turns of the "Where are you?" game and the dog will understand that everyone is playing the game and that each person has a big celebration awaiting the dog's success at locating him or her. Once the dog learns to love the game, simply calling out "Where are you?" will bring him running from wherever he is when he hears that all-important question.

The come command is recognized as one of the most important things to teach a dog, but there are trainers who work with thousands of dogs and never teach the actual word "come." Yet these dogs will race to respond to a person who uses the dog's name followed by "Where are you?" For example, a woman has a 12-year-old companion dog who went blind, but who never fails to locate her owner when asked, "Where are you?"

Children, in particular, love to play this game with their dogs. Children can hide in smaller places like a shower or bath tub, behind a bed or under a table. The dog needs to work a little bit harder to find these hiding places, but, when he does, he loves to celebrate with a treat and a tussle with a favorite youngster.

THE HEEL EXERCISE

Heeling means that the dog walks beside the owner without pulling. It takes time and patience on the owner's part to succeed at teaching the dog that he (the owner) will not proceed unless the dog is walking calmly beside him. Neither pulling out ahead on the lead nor lagging behind is acceptable.

Begin by holding the lead in your left hand as the dog sits beside your left leg. Move the loop end of the lead to your right hand, but keep your left hand short on the lead so that it keeps the dog in close next to you.

Say "Heel" and step forward on your left foot. Keep the dog close to you and take three steps. Stop and have the dog sit next to you in what we now call the heel position. Praise verbally, but do not touch the dog. Hesitate a moment and begin again with "Heel," taking three steps and stopping, at which point the dog is told to sit again.

Your goal here is to have the dog walk those three steps without pulling on the lead. Once he will walk calmly beside you for three steps without

TUG OF WALK?

If you begin teaching the heel by taking long walks and letting the dog pull you along, he misinterprets this action as an acceptable form of taking a walk. When you pull back on the lead to counteract his pulling, he reads that tug as a signal to pull even harder!

pulling, increase the number of steps you take to five. When he will walk politely beside you while you take five steps, you can increase the length of your walk to ten steps. Keep increasing the length of your stroll until the dog will walk quietly beside you without pulling as long as you want him to heel. When you stop heeling, indicate to the dog that the exercise is over by verbally praising as you pet him and say, "OK, good dog." The "OK" is used as a release word, meaning that the exercise is finished and the dog is free to relax.

If you are dealing with a dog who insists on pulling you around, simply "put on your brakes" and stand your ground until the dog realizes that the two of you are not going anywhere until he is beside you and moving at your pace, not his. It may take some time just standing there to convince the dog that you are the leader and that you will be the

one to decide on the direction and speed of your travel.

Each time the dog looks up at you or slows down to give a slack lead between the two of you, quietly praise him and say, "Good heel. Good dog." Eventually, the dog will begin to respond and within a few days he will be walking politely beside you without pulling on the lead. At first, the training sessions should be kept short and very positive; soon the dog will be able to walk nicely with you for increasingly

Train your puppy in an area where there are limited distractions. This puppy seems more interested in the tennis ball than in the sit-stay exercise that's being practiced.

SAFETY FIRST

While it may seem that the most important things to your dog are eating, sleeping and chewing the upholstery on your furniture, his first concern is actually safety. The domesticated dogs we keep as companions have the same pack instinct as their ancestors who ran free thousands of years ago. Because of this pack instinct, your dog wants to know that he and his pack are not in danger of being harmed, and that his pack has a strong, capable leader. You must establish yourself as the leader early on in your relationship. That way your dog will trust that you will take care of him and the pack, and he will accept your commands without question.

longer distances. Remember also to give the dog free time and the opportunity to run and play when you have finished heel practice.

WEANING OFF FOOD IN TRAINING

Food is used in training new behaviors. Once the dog understands what behavior goes with a specific command, it is time to start weaning him off the food treats. At first, give a treat after each exercise. Then, start to give a treat only after every other exercise. Mix up the times when you offer a food reward and the times when you only offer praise so that the dog will never know when he is going to receive both food and praise and when he is going to receive only praise. This is called a variable ratio reward system. It proves successful because there is always the chance that the owner will produce a treat, so the dog never stops trying for that reward. No matter what, *always* give verbal praise.

OBEDIENCE CLASSES

It is a good idea to enroll in an obedience class if one is available in your area. If yours is a show dog, handling classes would be more appropriate. Many areas have dog clubs that offer basic obedience training as well as preparatory classes for obedience competition. There are also local dog trainers who offer similar classes.

At obedience events, dogs can earn titles at various levels of competition. The beginning levels of obedience competition include basic behaviors such as sit, down, heel, etc. The more advanced levels of competition include jumping, retrieving, scent discrimination and signal work. The advanced levels require a dog and owner to put a lot of time and effort into their training. The titles that can be earned at these levels of competition are very prestigious.

OTHER ACTIVITIES FOR LIFE

Whether a dog is trained in the structured environment of a class or alone with his owner at home, there are many activities that can bring fun and rewards to both owner and dog once they have mastered basic control.

Teaching the dog to help out around the home, in the yard or on the farm provides great satisfaction to both dog and owner. In addition, the dog's help makes life a little easier for his owner and raises his stature as a valued companion to his family. It helps give the dog a purpose by occupying his mind and providing an outlet for his energy.

Backpacking is an exciting and healthy activity that the dog can be taught without assistance from more than his owner. The

FEAR AGGRESSION

Pups who are subjected to physical abuse during training commonly end up with behavioral problems as adults. One common result of abuse is fear aggression, in which a dog will lash out, bare his teeth, snarl and finally bite someone by whom he feels threatened. For example, your daughter may be playing with the dog one afternoon. As they play hide-and-seek, she backs the dog into a corner and, as she attempts to tease him playfully, he bites her hand. Examine the cause of this behavior. Did your daughter ever hit the dog? Did someone who resembles your daughter hit or scream at the dog?

Fortunately, fear aggression is relatively easy to correct. Have your daughter engage in only positive activities with the dog, such as feeding, petting and walking. She should not give any corrections or negative feedback. If the dog still growls or cowers away from her, allow someone else to accompany them. After approximately one week, the dog should feel that he can rely on her for many positive things, and he will also be prevented from reacting fearfully towards anyone who might resemble her.

exercise of walking and climbing is good for man and dog alike, and the bond that they develop together is priceless. The rule for backpacking with any dog is never to expect the dog to carry more than one-sixth of his body weight.

If you are interested in participating in organized competition with your Presa, there are activities other than obedience in which you and your dog can become involved. Agility is a popular sport in which dogs run through an obstacle course that includes various jumps, tunnels and other exercises to test the dog's speed and coordination. The owners run beside their dogs to give commands and to guide them through the course. Although competitive, the focus is on fun— it's fun to do, fun to watch and great exercise.

As a Presa owner, you have the opportunity to participate in Schutzhund competition if you choose. Schutzhund originated as a test to determine the best-quality dogs to be used for breeding stock. Breeders continue to use it as a way to evaluate working ability and temperament. Schutzhund should not be mistaken for attack training. While sleeve work is a part of Schutzhund, it is not the main focus of the discipline.

There are three levels in Schutzhund trials: SchH. I, SchH. II and SchH. III, with each level being progressively more difficult to complete successfully. Each level consists of training, obedience and protection phases. Training for Schutzhund is intense and must be practiced consistently to keep the dog keen. The experience of Schutzhund training is very rewarding for dog and owner, and the Presa's tractability is well suited for this type of training.

PERRO DE PRESA CANARIO

As a Presa Canario owner, you have selected your dog so that you and your loved ones can have a protector, a working dog, a companion and a four-legged family member. You invest time, money and effort to care for and train the family's new charge. Of course, this chosen canine behaves perfectly! Well, perfectly like a *dog.*

THINK LIKE A DOG

Dogs do not think like humans, nor do humans think like dogs, though we try. However, never try to "humanize" a dog. Unfortunately, a dog is incapable of comprehending how humans think, so the responsibility falls on the owner to adopt a proper canine mindset. Dogs cannot rationalize, and dogs exist in the present moment. Many a dog owner makes the mistake in training of thinking that he can reprimand his dog for something the dog did a while ago. Basically, you cannot even reprimand a dog for something he did 20 seconds ago! Either catch him in the act or forget it! It is a waste of your and your dog's time—in his mind, you are reprimanding him for whatever he is doing at that moment.

The following behavioral problems represent some which owners most commonly encounter. Every dog is unique and every situation is unique. No author could purport for you to solve your Presa's problems simply by reading a script. Here we outline some basic "dogspeak" so that owners' chances of solving behavioral problems are increased.

Discuss bad habits with your vet and he can recommend a behavioral specialist to consult in appropriate cases. Since behavioral abnormalities are the main reason for owners' abandoning their pets, we hope that you will make a valiant effort to solve your Presa's problems. Patience and understanding are virtues that must dwell in every pet-loving household.

AGGRESSION

This is a problem that concerns all responsible dog owners, and Presa owners are particularly concerned. Aggression can be a very big problem in dogs, and, when not controlled, always becomes dangerous. Unless untrained or improperly trained, a Presa is not a "dangerous dog." A dog with a fighting-dog background can be naturally aggressive toward other dogs, though should never be aggressive toward humans. Presas were trained to protect, not to attack, humans.

Aggressive behavior, such as lunging at a human, is not to be tolerated in any animal. While not all aggressive behavior is dangerous, growling, baring teeth, etc., can be frightening. It is important to ascertain why the dog is acting in this manner. Aggression is a display of dominance, and the dog should not have the dominant role in its pack, which is, in this case, your family.

It is important not to challenge an aggressive dog, as this could provoke an attack. Observe your Presa's body language. Does he make direct eye contact and stare? Does he try to make himself as large as possible: ears pricked, chest out, tail erect? Height and size signify authority in a dog pack—being taller or "above" another dog literally means that he is "above" in social status. These body signals tell you that your Presa thinks he is in charge, a problem that needs to be addressed. An aggressive dog is unpredictable; you never know

when he is going to strike and what he is going to do. You cannot understand why a dog that is playful one minute is growling the next.

Fear is a common cause of aggression in dogs. Perhaps your Presa had a negative experience as a puppy, which causes him to be fearful when a similar situation presents itself later in life. The dog may act aggressively in order to protect himself from whatever is making him afraid. It is not always easy to determine what is making your dog fearful, but if you can isolate what brings out the fear reaction, you can help the dog get over it.

Supervise your Presa's interactions with people and other dogs, and praise the dog when it goes well. If he starts to act aggressively in a situation, correct him and remove him from the situation. Do not let people approach the dog and start petting him without your express permission. That way, you can have the dog sit to accept petting, and praise him when he behaves properly. You are focusing on praise and on modifying his behavior by rewarding him when he acts appropriately. By being gentle and by supervising his interactions, you are showing him that there is no need to be afraid or defensive.

The best solution is to consult a behavioral specialist, one who has experience with the Presa (or similar breeds) if possible. Together, perhaps you can pinpoint the cause of your dog's aggression and do something about it. An aggressive dog cannot be trusted, and a dog that cannot be trusted is not safe to have as a family pet. If, very unusually, you find that your pet has become untrustworthy and you feel it necessary to seek a new home with a more suitable family and environment, explain fully to the new owners all your reasons for rehoming the dog to be fair to all concerned. In the very worst case, you will have to consider euthanasia.

AGGRESSION TOWARD OTHER DOGS
Whether a Presa Canario or a Pomeranian, a dog's aggressive behavior toward another dog stems from not enough exposure to other dogs at an early age. Socialization is key when dealing with a potentially dog-aggressive breed like the Presa. The Presa, as a breed with a fighting-dog background, does not readily accept strange dogs, and naturally will be quarrelsome with dogs of his/her same sex. If other dogs make your Presa nervous and agitated, he will lash out to show his fearlessness or even his insecurity. A dog that has not received sufficient exposure to other canines tends to think that he is the only dog on the island. The animal becomes so dominant that he does not even show signs that he is fearful or threatened. Without growling or any other physical signal as a warning, he will lunge at and bite the other dog.

A way to correct this is to let your Presa approach another dog when walking on lead. Watch very closely and, at the first sign of aggression, correct your Presa and pull him away. Scold him for any sign of discomfort, and then praise him when he ignores the other dog. Keep this up until either he stops the aggressive behavior, learns to ignore other dogs or even accepts other dogs. Praise him lavishly for this correct behavior.

DOMINANT AGGRESSION
A social hierarchy is firmly established in a wild dog pack. The dog wants to dominate those under him and please those above him. Dogs know that there must be a leader. If you are not the obvious choice for emperor, the dog will assume the throne! These conflicting innate desires are what a dog owner is up against when he sets about training a dog. In training a dog to obey commands, the owner is reinforcing that he is the top dog in the pack and that the dog should, and should want to, serve his superior. Thus, the owner is suppressing the dog's urge to dominate by modifying his behavior and making him obedient.

An important part of training is taking every opportunity to reinforce that you are the leader. The simple action of making your Presa sit to wait for his food instead of allowing him to run up to get it when he wants it says that you control when he eats; he is dependent on you for food. Although it may be difficult, do not give in to your dog's wishes every time he whines at you or looks at you with pleading eyes. It is a constant effort to show the dog that his place in the pack is at the bottom. This is not meant to sound cruel or inhumane. You love your Presa and you should treat him with care and affection. You (hopefully) did not get a dog just so you could control another creature. Dog training is not about being cruel or feeling important, it is about molding the dog's behavior into what is acceptable and teaching him to live by your rules.

In theory, it is quite simple: catch your Presa in appropriate behavior and reward him for it. Add a dog into the equation and it becomes a bit more trying, but, as a rule of thumb, positive reinforcement is what works best.

With a dominant dog, punishment and negative reinforcement can have the opposite effect of what you are after. It can make a dog fearful and/or act out aggressively if he feels he is being challenged. Remember, a domin-

NO EYE CONTACT

DANGER! If you and your on-lead dog are approached by a larger, running dog that is not restrained, walk away from the dog as calmly and quickly as possible. Do not allow your dog to make eye contact with the other dog. You should not make eye contact either. In dog terms, eye contact indicates a challenge.

ant dog perceives himself at the top of the social heap, and will fight to defend his perceived status. The best way to prevent that is to never give your dog reason to think that he is in control in the first place.

If you are having trouble training your Presa and it seems

as if he is constantly challenging your authority, seek the help of an obedience trainer or behavioral specialist. A professional will work with both you and your dog to teach you effective techniques to use at home. Beware of trainers who rely on excessively harsh methods; scolding is necessary now and then, but the focus in your training should always be on positive reinforcement.

SEPARATION ANXIETY

Recognized by behaviorists as the most common form of stress for dogs, separation anxiety can also lead to destructive behaviors in your dog. It's more than your Presa's howling his displeasure at your leaving the house and his being left alone. This is a normal reaction, no different from the child who cries as his mother leaves him on the first day at school. Separation anxiety is more serious. In fact, if you are constantly with your dog, he will come to expect you with him all of the time, making it even more traumatic for him when you are not there.

Obviously, you enjoy spending time with your dog, and he thrives on your love and attention. However, it should not become a dependent relationship in which he is heartbroken without you. This broken heart can also bring on destructive behavior as well as loss of

appetite, depression and lack of interest in play and interaction. Canine behaviorists have been spending much time and energy to help owners better understand the significance of this stressful condition.

One thing you can do to minimize separation anxiety is to make your entrances and exits as low-key as possible. Do not give your dog a long drawn-out goodbye, and do not lavish him with hugs and kisses when you return. This is giving in to the attention that he craves, and it will only make him miss it more when you are away. Another thing you can try is to give your dog a treat when you leave; this will not only keep him occupied and keep his mind off the fact that you have just left, but it will also help him associate your leaving with a pleasant experience.

You may have to accustom your dog to being left alone in intervals. Of course, when your dog starts whimpering as you approach the door, your first instinct will be to run to him and comfort him, but do not do it! Eventually he will adjust to your absence. His anxiety stems from being placed in an unfamiliar situation; by familiarizing him with being alone, he will learn that he will survive. That is not to say you should purposely leave your dog home alone, but the dog needs to know that, while he can depend on you for his care, you do not have to be by his side 24 hours a day. Some behaviorists recommend tiring the dog out before you leave home—take him for a good long walk or engage in a game of fetch in the yard.

When the dog is alone in the house, he should be placed in his crate—another distinct advantage to crate training your dog. The crate should be placed in his familiar happy family area, where he normally sleeps and already feels comfortable, thereby making him feel more at ease when he is alone. Be sure to give the dog a special chew toy to enjoy while he settles into his crate.

SEXUAL BEHAVIOR

Dogs exhibit certain sexual behaviors that may have influenced your choice of male or female when you first purchased your Presa. To a certain extent, spaying/neutering will eliminate these behaviors, but if you are purchasing a dog that you wish to breed from, you should be aware of what you will have to deal with throughout the dog's life.

Female dogs usually have two estruses per year, with each season lasting about three weeks. These are the only times in which a female dog will mate, and she usually will not allow this until the second week of the cycle, although this varies from bitch to bitch. If not bred during the heat

cycle, it is not uncommon for a bitch to experience a false pregnancy, in which her mammary glands swell and she exhibits maternal tendencies toward toys or other objects.

With male dogs, owners must be aware that whole dogs (dogs who are not neutered) have the natural inclination to mark their territory. Males mark their territory by spraying small amounts of urine as they lift their legs in a macho ritual. Marking can occur both outdoors in the yard and around the neighborhood as well as indoors on furniture legs, curtains and the couch. Such behavior can be very frustrating for the owner; early training is strongly urged before the "urge" strikes your dog. Neutering the male at an appropriate early age can solve this problem before it becomes a habit.

Other problems associated with males are wandering and mounting. Both of these habits, of course, belong to the unneutered dog, whose sexual drive leads him away from home in search of the bitch in heat. Males will mount females in heat, as well as any other dog, male or female, that happens to catch their fancy. Other possible mounting partners include his owner, the furniture, guests to the home and people on the street. Discourage such behavior early on.

Owners must further recognize that mounting is not merely a sexual expression but also one of dominance that can be seen in both males and females. Be consistent and be persistent, and you will find that you can "move mounters."

CHEWING
The national canine pastime is chewing! Every dog loves to sink his "canines" into a tasty bone, but if a bone isn't available, he'll find somewhere else to sink his teeth. Dogs need to chew, to massage their gums, to make their new teeth feel better and to exercise their jaws. This is a natural behavior that is deeply embedded in all things canine. Our role as owners is not to stop the dog's chewing, but rather to redirect it to positive, chew-worthy objects. Be an informed owner and purchase proper chew toys, like strong nylon bones, that will not splinter. Be sure that the objects are safe and durable, since your dog's safety is at risk. Again, the owner is responsible for ensuring a dog-proof environment.

The best answer is prevention; that is, put your shoes, handbags and other tasty objects in their proper places (out of the reach of the growing canine mouth). Direct puppies to their toys whenever you see them "tasting" the furniture legs or the leg of your pants. Make a loud noise to attract the pup's attention and immediately escort him to his chew toy and engage him with the toy for at least four minutes, praising and encouraging him all the while. An array of safe, interesting chew toys will keep your dog's mind and teeth occupied, and distracted from chewing on things he shouldn't.

Some trainers recommend deterrents, such as hot pepper, a bitter spice or a product designed for this purpose, to discourage the dog from chewing unwanted objects. Test these products to see which works best before investing in large quantities.

JUMPING UP
Jumping up is a dog's friendly way of saying hello! Some dog owners do not mind when their dog jumps up. The problem arises when guests come to the house and the dog greets them in the same manner—whether they like it or not! However friendly the

NO JUMPING
Stop a dog from jumping up before he jumps. If he is getting ready to jump onto you, simply walk away. If he jumps up on you before you can turn away, lift your knee so that it bumps him in the chest. Do not be forceful. Your dog soon will realize that jumping up is not a good way of getting attention.

greeting may be, the chances are that your visitors will not appreciate this type of enthusiastic hello from a dog as large as the Presa. The dog will not be able to distinguish upon whom he can jump and whom he cannot. Therefore, it is probably best to discourage this behavior entirely.

Pick a command such as "Off" (avoid using "Down" since you will use that for the dog to lie down) and tell him "Off" when he jumps up. Place him on the ground on all fours and have him sit, praising him the whole time. Always lavish him with praise and petting when he is in the sit position. In this way, you can give him a warm affectionate greeting, let him know that you are as pleased to see him as he is to see you and instill good manners at the same time!

DIGGING
Digging, which is seen as a destructive behavior to humans, is actually quite a natural behavior in dogs. Although terriers (the "earth dogs") are most associated with the digging, any dog's desire to dig can be irrepressible and most frustrating to his owners. When digging occurs in your garden, it is actually a normal behavior redirected into something the dog can do in his everyday life. In the wild, a dog would be actively seeking food, making his own shelter, etc. He

would be using his paws in a purposeful manner for his survival. Since you provide him with food and shelter, he has no need to use his paws for these purposes, and so the energy that he would be using may manifest itself in the form of little holes all over your yard and flower garden.

Perhaps your dog is digging as a reaction to boredom—it is somewhat similar to someone eating a whole bag of chips in front of the TV—because they are there and there is nothing better to do! Basically, the answer is to provide the dog with adequate

While you may welcome an enthusiastic greeting from a puppy, you'll likely feel differently if 100 lbs. of Presa jumps up to say hello! Discourage jumping up early in the dog's life.

play and exercise so that his mind and paws are occupied, and so that he feels as if he is doing something useful.

Of course, digging is easiest to control if it is stopped as soon as possible, but it is often hard to catch a dog in the act. If your dog is a compulsive digger and is not easily distracted by other activities, you can designate an area on your property where he is allowed to dig. If you catch him digging in an off-limits area of the yard,

immediately bring him to the approved area and praise him for digging there. Keep a close eye on him so that you can catch him in the act—that is the only way to make him understand what is permitted and what is not. If you take him to a hole he dug an hour ago and tell him "No," he will understand that you are not fond of holes, dirt or flowers. If you catch him while he is stifle-deep in your tulips, that is when he will get your message.

BARKING

Blest with a deep, sonorous bark, the Presa Canario uses his bark purposefully in his duty of protecting his family and property. When the Presa is a puppy, the owner must communicate clearly to the dog when his barking is appropriate and necessary versus when it is simply a nuisance. If an intruder came into your home in the middle of the night and your Presa barked a warning, you would praise the dog and tell him "Good dog." You would deem your dog a hero, a wonderful protector of the home, and he should understand your feelings. On the other hand, if a friend walks up to your gate and is greeted with constant barking, you should tell the dog "OK," so that he knows that there is no danger and no need to continue barking.

For a dog without training, both scenarios are the same. The

DOG TALK

Deciphering your dog's barks is very similar to understanding a baby's cries: there is a different cry for eating, sleeping, potty needs, etc. Your dog talks to you not only through howls and groans but also through his body language. Baring teeth, staring and inflating the chest are all threatening gestures. If a dog greets you by licking his nose, turning his head or yawning, these are friendly, peacemaking gestures.

dog does not know any better. While your friend is not posing a threat, it is all the same to the dog. Barking is his means of letting you know that there is an intrusion, whether friend or foe, on your property. This type of barking is instinctive and should not be discouraged, but the dog should be trained to stop barking at your command.

Excessive habitual barking, however, is a problem that should be corrected early on. As your Presa grows up, you will be able to tell when his barking is purposeful and when it is for no reason. You will become able to distinguish your dog's different barks and their meanings. For example, the bark when someone comes to the door will be different from the bark when he is excited to see you. It is similar to a person's tone of voice, except that the dog has to rely totally on tone of voice because he does not have the benefit of using words. An incessant barker will be evident at an early age.

There are some things that encourage a dog to bark. For example, if your dog barks non-stop for a few minutes and you give him a treat to quiet him, he believes that you are rewarding him for barking. He will associate barking with getting a treat, and will keep doing it until he is rewarded. On the other hand, if you give him a command such as

"Quiet" or "OK" and praise him after he has stopped barking for a few seconds, he will get the idea that being "quiet" is what you want him to do.

FOOD STEALING

Is your dog devising ways of stealing food from your coffee table or kitchen counter? If so, you must answer the following questions: Is your Presa hungry, or is he "constantly famished" like many dogs seem to be? Face it, some dogs are more food-motivated than others. They are totally obsessed by the smell of food and can only think of their next meal. Food stealing is terrific fun and always yields a great reward—FOOD, glorious food.

Your goal as an owner, therefore, is to be sensible about where food is placed in the home and to reprimand your dog whenever he is caught in the act of stealing. But remember, only reprimand your dog if you actually see him stealing, not later when the crime is discovered; that will be of no use at all and will only serve to confuse him.

BEGGING

Just like food stealing, begging is a favorite pastime of hungry puppies! It achieves that same terrific result—FOOD! Dogs quickly learn that their owners keep the "good food" for themselves, and that we humans do not dine on dry food alone. Begging is a conditioned response related to a specific stimulus, time and place. The sounds of the kitchen, cans and bottles opening, crinkling bags, the smell of food in preparation, etc., will excite the dog, and soon the paws will be in the air!

Here is the solution to stopping this behavior: Never give in to a beggar! You are rewarding the dog for sitting pretty, jumping up, whining and rubbing his nose into you by giving him food. By ignoring the dog, you will (eventually) force the behavior into extinction. Note that the behavior is likely to get worse before it disappears, so be sure there are not any "softies" in the family who will give in to little "Olivero" every time he whimpers, *"Más, por favor."*

COPROPHAGIA
Feces eating is, to humans, one of the most disgusting behaviors that their dogs could engage in, yet, to dogs, it is perfectly normal. It is hard for us to understand why a dog would want to eat his own feces. He could be seeking certain nutrients that are missing from his diet, he could be just plain hungry or he could be attracted by the pleasing (to a dog) scent. While coprophagia most often refers to the dog's eating his own feces, a dog may just as likely eat that of another animal as well if he

comes across it. Dogs often find the stool of cats and horses more palatable than that of other dogs.

Vets have found that diets with low levels of digestibility, containing relatively low levels of fiber and high levels of starch, increase coprophagia. Therefore, high-fiber diets may decrease the likelihood of dogs' eating feces. Both the consistency of the stool (how firm it feels in the dog's mouth) and the presence of undigested nutrients increase the likelihood. Once the dog develops diarrhea from feces eating, he will likely stop this distasteful habit.

To discourage this behavior, first make sure that the food you are feeding your dog is nutritionally complete and that he is getting enough food. If changes in his diet do not seem to work, and no medical cause can be found, you will have to modify the behavior through environmental control before it becomes a habit. The best way to prevent your dog from eating his stool is to make it unavailable—clean up after he eliminates and remove any stool from the yard. If it is not there, he cannot eat it.

Reprimanding for stool eating rarely impresses the dog. Vets recommend distracting the dog while he is in the act of stool eating. Coprophagia is seen most frequently in pups 6 to 12 months of age, and usually disappears around the dog's first birthday.

HEALTH CARE OF YOUR
PERRO DE PRESA CANARIO

Dogs suffer from many of the same physical illnesses as people. Since people usually know more about human diseases than canine maladies, many of the terms used in this chapter will be familiar but not necessarily those used by vets. We will use the term *x-ray*, instead of the more acceptable term *radiograph*. We will also use the familiar term *symptoms* even though dogs don't have symptoms, which are verbal descriptions of the patient's feelings; dogs have *clinical signs*. Since dogs can't speak, we have to look for clinical signs...but we still use the term *symptoms* in this book.

As a general rule, medicine is *practiced*. That term is not arbitrary. Medicine is a constantly changing art as we learn more and more about genetics, electronic aids (like CAT scans and MRIs) and daily laboratory advances. There are many dog maladies, like canine hip dysplasia, which are not universally treated in the same manner. Some vets opt for surgery more often than others do.

SELECTING A QUALIFIED VET

Your selection of a vet should not be based solely upon personality (as most are) but also upon his skills, especially with large-breed dogs, and his convenience to your home. You want a vet who is close because you might have emergencies or need to make multiple visits for treatments. You want a vet who has services that you might require such as tattooing and boarding, as well as sophisticated pet supplies and a good reputation for ability and responsiveness. There is nothing more frustrating than having to wait a day or more to get a response from your vet.

All vets are licensed and their diplomas and/or certificates should be displayed in their waiting rooms. There are, however, many veterinary specialties that usually require further studies and internships. There are specialists in heart problems (veterinary cardiologists), skin problems (veterinary dermatologists), teeth and gum problems (veterinary dentists), eye problems

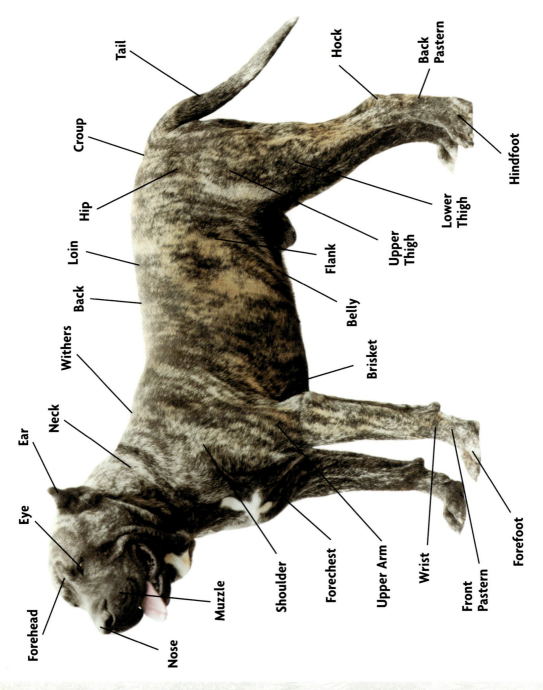

Tail

Croup

Hock

Back Pastern

Hindfoot

Hip

Lower Thigh

Upper Thigh

Loin

Flank

Back

Belly

Withers

Brisket

Neck

Ear

Eye

Wrist

Forehead

Front Pastern

Forefoot

Nose

Muzzle

Shoulder

Forechest

Upper Arm

PHYSICAL STRUCTURE OF THE PERRO DE PRESA CANARIO

(veterinary ophthalmologists) and x-rays (veterinary radiologists), as well as vets who have specialties in bones, muscles or certain organs. Most vets do routine surgery such as neutering, stitching up wounds and docking tails for those breeds in which such is required for show purposes.

When the problem affecting your dog is serious, it is not unusual to get another medical opinion, and it is polite to advise the vets concerned about this. You might also want to compare costs among several vets. Sophisticated health care and veterinary services can be very costly. It is not infrequent that important decisions about the course of treatment to take are based upon financial considerations.

PREVENTATIVE MEDICINE

It is much easier, less costly and more effective to practice preventative medicine than to fight bouts of illness and disease. Properly bred puppies come from parents who were selected based upon their genetic-disease profiles. Their dam should have been

CUSHING'S DISEASE

Cases of hyperactive adrenal glands (Cushing's disease) have been traced to the drinking of highly chlorinated water. Aerate or age your dog's drinking water before offering it.

Breakdown of Veterinary Income by Category

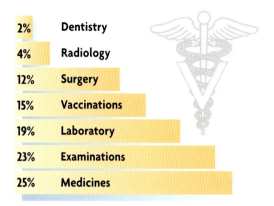

2%	Dentistry
4%	Radiology
12%	Surgery
15%	Vaccinations
19%	Laboratory
23%	Examinations
25%	Medicines

A typical vet's income, categorized according to services performed. This survey dealt with small-animal (pets) practices.

vaccinated, free of all internal and external parasites and properly nourished. The dam can pass on disease resistance to her puppies, which can last for eight to ten weeks, but she can also pass on parasites and many infections. For these reasons, a visit to the vet who cared for the dam is recommended to learn more about her health.

VACCINATION SCHEDULING

Most vaccinations are given by injection and should only be done by a veterinarian. Both he and you should keep records of the date of the injection, the identification of the vaccine and the amount given. Some vets give a first vaccination at eight weeks, but most dog breeders prefer the course not to commence until about ten weeks to avoid negating any antibodies passed on by the dam. The vaccination scheduling is usually

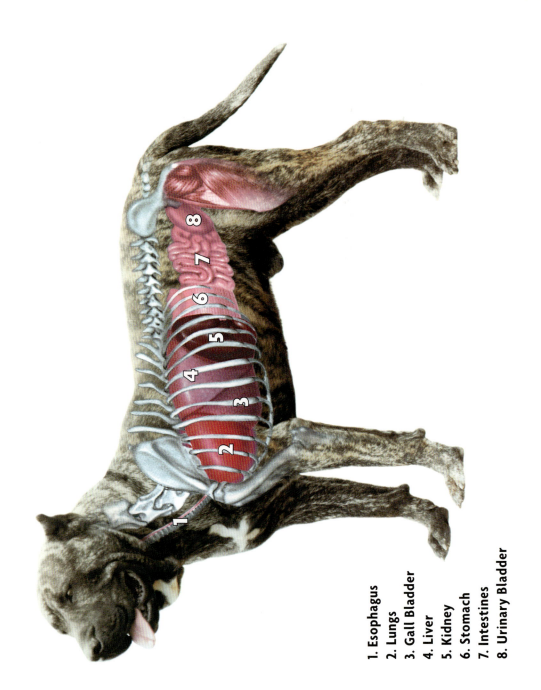

1. Esophagus
2. Lungs
3. Gall Bladder
4. Liver
5. Kidney
6. Stomach
7. Intestines
8. Urinary Bladder

INTERNAL ORGANS OF THE PERRO DE PRESA CANARIO

HEALTH AND VACCINATION SCHEDULE

AGE IN WEEKS:	6TH	8TH	10TH	12TH	14TH	16TH	20-24TH	52ND
Worm Control	✔	✔	✔	✔	✔	✔	✔	
Neutering								✔
Heartworm		✔		✔		✔	✔	
Parvovirus	✔		✔		✔		✔	✔
Distemper		✔		✔		✔		✔
Hepatitis		✔		✔		✔		✔
Leptospirosis								✔
Parainfluenza	✔		✔		✔			✔
Dental Examination		✔					✔	✔
Complete Physical		✔					✔	✔
Coronavirus				✔			✔	✔
Kennel Cough	✔							
Hip Dysplasia								✔
Rabies							✔	

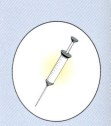

Vaccinations are not instantly effective. It takes about two weeks for the dog's immune system to develop antibodies. Most vaccinations require annual booster shots. Your veterinarian should guide you in this regard.

based on a 15-day cycle. You must take your vet's advice regarding when to vaccinate, as this may differ according to the vaccine used.

VACCINE ALLERGIES

Vaccines do not work all the time. Sometimes dogs are allergic to them and many times the antibodies, which are supposed to be stimulated by the vaccine, just are not produced. You should keep your dog in the veterinary clinic for an hour after he is vaccinated to be sure there are no allergic reactions.

Most vaccinations immunize your puppy against viruses. The usual vaccines contain immunizing doses of several different viruses such as distemper, parvovirus, parainfluenza and hepatitis, although some vets recommend separate vaccines for each disease. There are other vaccines available when the puppy is at risk. You should rely upon professional advice. This is especially true for the booster-shot program. Most vaccination programs require a booster when the puppy is a year old and once a year thereafter. In some cases,

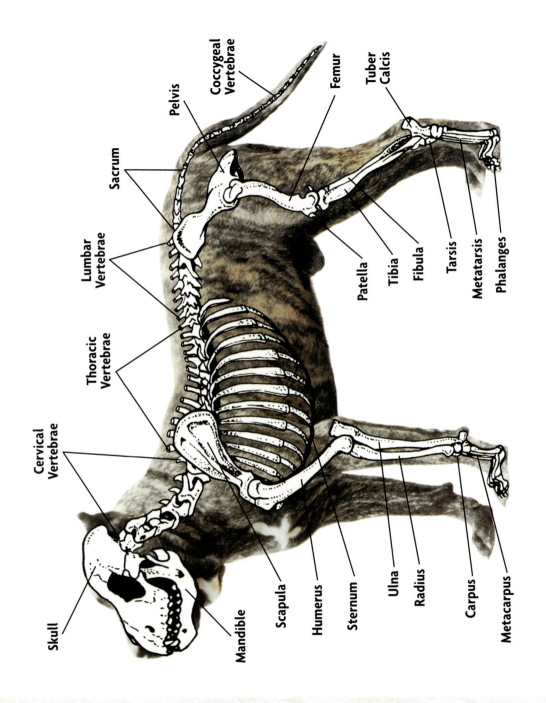

Coccygeal Vertebrae

Pelvis

Femur

Tuber Calcis

Sacrum

Patella

Tibia

Fibula

Tarsis

Metatarsis

Phalanges

Lumbar Vertebrae

Thoracic Vertebrae

Cervical Vertebrae

Skull

Mandible

Scapula

Humerus

Sternum

Ulna

Radius

Carpus

Metacarpus

SKELETAL STRUCTURE OF THE PERRO DE PRESA CANARIO

circumstances may require more or less frequent immunizations. Kennel cough, more formally known as tracheobronchitis, is treated with a vaccine that is sprayed into the dog's nostrils. Kennel cough is usually included in routine vaccination, but this is often not as effective as the vaccines for other major diseases.

WEANING TO FIVE MONTHS OLD
Puppies should be weaned by the time they are about two months old. A puppy that remains for at least eight weeks with his mother and littermates usually adapts better to other dogs and people later in life. Some new owners have their puppies examined by vets immediately, which is a good idea. Vaccination programs usually begin when the puppy is very young.

The puppy will have his teeth examined, and have his skeletal conformation and general health checked prior to certification by the vet. Puppies in certain breeds may have problems with their kneecaps, cataracts and other eye problems, heart murmurs and undescended testicles. They may also have personality problems, and your vet might have training in temperament evaluation.

FIVE TO TWELVE MONTHS OF AGE
Unless you intend to breed or show your dog, neutering the

BE CAREFUL WHERE YOU WALK YOUR DOG
Dogs who have been exposed to lawns sprayed with herbicides have double and triple the rate of malignant lymphoma. Suburban dogs are especially at risk, as they are exposed to manicured lawns and gardens. Dogs perspire and absorb through their footpads. Be careful where your dog walks and always avoid any area that appears yellowed from chemical overspray. These chemicals are not good for you, either!

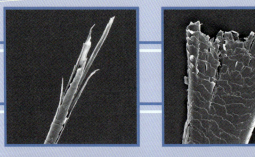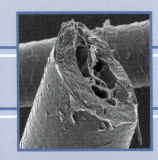

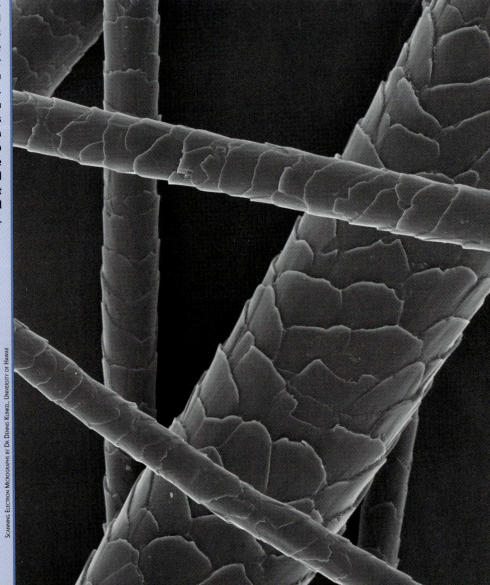

Normal hairs of a dog enlarged 200 times original size. The cuticle (outer covering) is clean and healthy. Unlike human hair that grows from the base, a dog's hair also grows from the end. Damaged hairs and split ends, illustrated above.

puppy at six months of age is recommended. Discuss this with your vet. Neutering/spaying has proven to be extremely beneficial to male and female puppies, respectively. Besides eliminating the possibility of pregnancy, it inhibits (but does not prevent) breast cancer in bitches and prostate cancer in male dogs. Under no circumstances should a bitch be spayed prior to her first season.

Your vet should provide your puppy with a thorough dental evaluation at six months of age, ascertaining whether all the permanent teeth have erupted properly. A home dental-care regimen should be initiated at six months, including brushing weekly and providing good dental devices (such as nylon bones). Regular dental care promotes healthy teeth, fresh breath and a longer life.

NEUTERING/SPAYING
Male dogs are castrated. The operation removes both testicles and requires that the dog be anesthetized. Recovery takes about one week. Females are spayed; in this operation, the uterus (womb) and both of the ovaries are removed. This is major surgery, also carried out under general anesthesia, and it usually takes a bitch two weeks to recover.

MORE THAN VACCINES
Vaccinations help prevent your new puppy from contracting diseases, but they do not cure them. Proper nutrition as well as parasite control keep your dog healthy and less susceptible to many dangerous diseases. Remember that your dog depends on you to ensure his well-being.

ONE YEAR AND OLDER
Once a year, your grown dog should visit the vet for an examination and vaccination boosters, if needed. Some vets recommend blood tests, a thyroid level check and a dental evaluation to accompany these annual visits. A thorough clinical evaluation by the vet can provide critical background information for your dog. Blood tests are often performed at one year of age, and dental examinations around the third or fourth birthday. In the long run, quality preventative care for your pet can save money, teeth and lives.

SKIN PROBLEMS IN PRESAS
Vets are consulted by dog owners for skin problems more than for any other group of diseases or maladies. Dogs' skin is almost as sensitive as human skin, and both suffer from almost the same ailments (though the occurrence of acne in most breeds of dog is rare!). For this reason, veterinary

dermatology has developed into a specialty practiced by many vets.

A common skin disorder in many breeds is demodectic mange, which affects the Presa during puppyhood, usually before 18 months of age. The condition is caused by the *Demodex canis* mite, a microscopic insect that exists on the skin of most dogs. Some dogs inherit an immuno-deficient susceptibility to these mites, and if hair loss is observed over the whole body, the condition is considered to be generalized.

Since many skin problems have visual symptoms that are almost identical, it requires the skill of an experienced veterinary dermatologist to identify and cure many of the more severe skin disorders. Pet shops sell many treatments for skin problems, but most of the treatments are directed at the symptoms and not the underlying problem(s). If your dog is suffering from a skin disorder, you should seek professional assistance as quickly as possible. As with all diseases, the earlier a problem is identified and treated, the more likely that the cure will be successful.

DISEASE REFERENCE CHART

	What is it?	What causes it?	Symptoms
Leptospirosis	Severe disease that affects the internal organs; can be spread to people.	A bacterium, which is often carried by rodents, that enters through mucous membranes and spreads quickly throughout the body.	Range from fever, vomiting and loss of appetite in less severe cases to shock, irreversible kidney damage and possibly death in most severe cases.
Rabies	Potentially deadly virus that infects warm-blooded mammals.	Bite from a carrier of the virus, mainly wild animals.	1st stage: dog exhibits change in behavior, fear. 2nd stage: dog's behavior becomes more aggressive. 3rd stage: loss of coordination, trouble with bodily functions.
Parvovirus	Highly contagious virus, potentially deadly.	Ingestion of the virus, which is usually spread through the feces of infected dogs.	Most common: severe diarrhea. Also vomiting, fatigue, lack of appetite.
Kennel cough	Contagious respiratory infection.	Combination of types of bacteria and virus. Most common: *Bordetella bronchiseptica* bacteria and parainfluenza virus.	Chronic cough.
Distemper	Disease primarily affecting respiratory and nervous system.	Virus that is related to the human measles virus.	Mild symptoms such as fever, lack of appetite and mucous secretion progress to evidence of brain damage, "hard pad."
Hepatitis	Virus primarily affecting the liver.	Canine adenovirus type I (CAV-1). Enters system when dog breathes in particles.	Lesser symptoms include listlessness, diarrhea, vomiting. More severe symptoms include "blue-eye" (clumps of virus in eye).
Coronavirus	Virus resulting in digestive problems.	Virus is spread through infected dog's feces.	Stomach upset evidenced by lack of appetite, vomiting, diarrhea.

PARASITE BITES

Many of us are allergic to insect bites. The bites itch, erupt and may even become infected. Dogs have the same reaction to fleas, ticks and/or mites. When an insect lands on you, you have the chance to whisk it away with your hand. Unfortunately, when your dog is bitten by a flea, tick or mite, he can only scratch it away or bite it. By the time the dog has been bitten, the parasite has done some of its damage. It may also have laid eggs, which will cause further problems in the near future. The itching from parasite bites is probably due to the saliva injected into the site when the parasite sucks the dog's blood.

ACRAL LICK GRANULOMA

Many large dogs have a very poorly understood syndrome called acral lick granuloma. The manifestation of the problem is the dog's tireless attack at a specific area of the body, almost always the legs or paws. The dog licks so intensively that he removes the hair and skin, leaving an ugly, large wound. Tiny protuberances, which are outgrowths of new capillaries, bead on the surface of the wound. Owners who notice their dogs' biting and chewing at their extremities should have the vet determine the cause. If lick granuloma is identified, although there is no absolute cure, corticos-

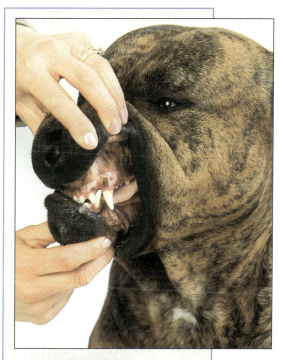

DENTAL HEALTH

A dental examination is in order when the dog is between six months and one year of age so that any permanent teeth that have erupted incorrectly can be corrected. It is important to begin a brushing routine at home, using a toothbrush and toothpaste made especially for canines. Durable nylon and safe edible chews should be a part of your puppy's arsenal for good health, good teeth and pleasant breath. The vast majority of dogs three to four years old and older has diseases of the gums from lack of dental attention. Using the various types of dental chews can be very effective in controlling dental plaque.

teroids are one common treatment. Your vet will advise you of the best course of action.

AIRBORNE ALLERGIES
Many dogs suffer from the same allergies as do humans, including various pollen allergies like hay fever and rose fever. When the pollen count is high, your dog might suffer, but don't expect him to sneeze and have a runny nose like a human would. Dogs react to pollen allergies the same way they react to fleas—they scratch and bite themselves. Dogs, like humans, can be tested for allergens. Discuss the testing with your veterinary dermatologist.

FOOD PROBLEMS

FOOD ALLERGIES
Dogs are allergic to many foods that are best-sellers and highly recommended by breeders and vets. Changing the brand of food that you buy may not eliminate the problem if the element to which the dog is allergic is also contained in the new brand.

Recognizing a food allergy is difficult. Humans vomit or have rashes when they eat a food to which they are allergic. Dogs neither vomit nor (usually) develop rashes. They react in the same manner as they would to an airborne or flea allergy; they itch, scratch and bite, thus making the diagnosis extremely difficult. While pollen allergies and parasite bites are usually seasonal, food allergies are year-round problems.

FOOD INTOLERANCE
Food intolerance is the inability of the dog to completely digest certain foods. Puppies that may

A puppy's curiosity can lead him to find unexpected problems, especially outdoors where molds, fungi and grasses can cause allergic reactions that are difficult to diagnose.

HOW TO PREVENT BLOAT

Research has confirmed that the structure of deep-chested breeds contributes to their predisposition to bloat. Nevertheless, there are precautions that you can take to reduce the risk of this condition:

- Feed your dog twice daily rather than offer one big meal.
- Do not exercise your dog for at least one hour before and two hours after he has eaten.
- Make certain that your dog is calm and not overly excited while he is eating. It has been proven that nervous or overly excited dogs are more prone to develop bloat.
- Add a small portion of moist meat product to his dry food ration.
- Serve his meals in an elevated bowl stand, which avoids the dog's craning his neck and swallowing air while eating.
- To prevent your dog from gobbling his food too quickly, and thereby swallowing air, put some large (unswallowable) toys into his bowl so that he will have to eat around them to get his food.

have done very well on their mother's milk may not do well on cows' milk. The results of food intolerance may be evident in loose bowels, passing gas and stomach pains. These are the only obvious symptoms of food intolerance, which makes diagnosis difficult.

TREATING FOOD PROBLEMS

It is possible to handle food allergies and food intolerance yourself. Start by putting your dog on a diet that he has never had. Obviously, if the dog has never eaten this new food, he can't have been allergic or intolerant of it. Start with a single ingredient that is not in the dog's diet at the present time. Ingredients like chopped beef or chicken are common in dogs' diets, so try a

diet with a source of protein like fish, rabbit or even something more exotic like pheasant. Keep the dog on this diet (with no additives) for a month. If the symptoms of food allergy or intolerance disappear, it is quite likely that your dog has a food allergy.

Don't think that the single ingredient cured the problem. You still must find a suitable diet and ascertain which ingredient in the old diet was objectionable. This is most easily done by adding ingredients to the new diet one at a time. Let the dog stay on the modified diet for a month before you add another ingredient. Eventually, you will determine the ingredient that caused the adverse reaction.

An alternative method is to

carefully study the ingredients in the diet to which your dog is allergic or intolerant. Identify the main ingredient in this diet and eliminate the main ingredient by buying a different food that does not have that ingredient. Keep experimenting until the symptoms disappear after one month on the new diet.

BLOAT OR GASTRIC TORSION

This is a problem found in the large, deep-chested breeds, and is the subject of much research, but still manages to kill many dogs before their time and in a very horrible way. Those breeds with the deepest chests are at the greatest risk of having their whole stomachs twist around (gastric torsion). This cuts off the blood supply and prevents the stomach's contents from leaving, and increases the amount of gas in the stomach. Once these things have happened, surgery is vital. If the blood supply has been cut off too long and a bit of the stomach wall dies, death of the Presa is almost inevitable.

The horrendous pain of this condition is due to the stomach wall's being stretched by the gas caught in the stomach, as well as the stomach wall's desperately needing the blood that cannot get to it. There is the pain of not being able to pass a much greater than normal amount of wind; added to this is a pain equivalent

A SKUNKY PROBLEM
Have you noticed your dog dragging his rump along the floor? If so, it is likely that his anal sacs are impacted or possibly infected. The anal sacs are small pouches located on both sides of the anus under the skin and muscles. They are about the size and shape of a grape and contain a foul-smelling liquid. Their contents are usually emptied when the dog has a bowel movement but, if not emptied completely, they will impact, which will cause your dog much pain. Fortunately, your veterinarian can tend to this problem easily by draining the sacs for the dog. Be aware that your dog might also empty his anal sacs in cases of extreme fright.

to that of a heart attack, which is due to the heart muscle's being starved of blood.

PREVENTING BLOAT

Here are some tips on how to reduce the risk of bloat in your Presa:
- Restrict exercise for at least one hour before meals;
- Restrict exercise for at least two hours after meals;
- Do not feed cheap food with high cereal content;
- Feed high-quality, low-residue diets;
- Elevate food and water bowls to try to reduce any air swallowed;
- If your Presa is greedy and eats

quickly, reduce the air swallowed by putting something large and inedible in the food bowl so that the dog has to pick around the object and thus eat more slowly.

DETECTING BLOAT
The following are symptoms of bloat and require immediate veterinary attention:
• Your dog's stomach starts to distend, ending up large and as tight as a basketball;

• Your dog is dribbling, as no saliva can be swallowed;
• Your dog makes frequent attempts to vomit but cannot bring anything up due to the stomach's being closed off;
• Your dog is distressed from pain;
• Your dog starts to suffer from clinical shock, meaning that there is not enough blood in the dog's circulation as the hard, dilated stomach stops the blood from returning to the heart to be pumped around the body. Clinical shock is indicated by pale gums and tongue, as they have been starved of blood. The shocked dog also has glazed, staring eyes.

You have minutes, yes *minutes*, to get your dog into surgery. If you see any of these symptoms at any time of the day or night, get to the vet's office immediately, as that is where all the equipment is located. Someone will have to phone and warn that you are on your way (which is a justification for the invention of the cell phone!), so that they can be prepared to get your pet on the operating table.

It is possible for a dog to have more than one incident of gastric torsion, even if it has had its stomach stapled, in which the stomach is stapled to the inside of the chest wall to give extra support and prevent its twisting again.

A male dog flea,
Ctenocephalides canis.

EXTERNAL PARASITES

FLEAS

Of all the problems to which dogs are prone, none is more well known and frustrating than fleas. Flea infestation is relatively simple to cure but difficult to prevent. Parasites that are harbored inside the body are a bit more difficult to eradicate but they are easier to control.

To control flea infestation, you have to understand the flea's life cycle. Fleas are often thought of as a summertime problem, but centrally heated homes have changed the patterns and fleas can be found at any time of the year.

The most effective method of flea control is a two-stage approach: one stage to kill the adult fleas, and the other to control the development of pre-adult fleas. Unfortunately, no single active ingredient is effective against all stages of the life cycle.

LIFE CYCLE STAGES

During its life, a flea will pass through four life stages: egg, larva, pupa and adult. The adult stage is the most visible and irritating stage of the flea life cycle, and this is why the majority of flea-control products concentrate on this stage. The fact is that adult fleas account for only 1% of the total flea population, and the other 99% exist in pre-adult stages, i.e. eggs, larvae and pupae. The pre-adult stages are barely visible to the naked eye.

THE LIFE CYCLE OF THE FLEA

Eggs are laid on the dog, usually in quantities of about 20 or 30, several times a day. The adult female flea must have a blood meal before each egg-laying session. When first laid, the eggs will cling to the dog's hair, as the eggs are still moist. However, they will quickly dry out and fall from the dog, especially if the dog moves around or scratches. Many eggs will fall off in the dog's favorite area or an area in which he spends a lot of time, such as his bed.

Once the eggs fall from the dog onto the carpet or furniture, they will hatch into larvae. This takes from one to ten days. Larvae are not particularly mobile and will usually travel only a few

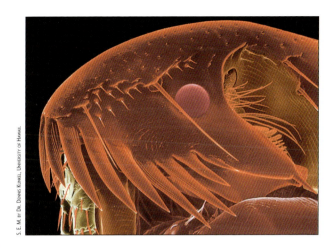

S. E. M. BY DR. DENNIS KUNKEL, UNIVERSITY OF HAWAII.

Magnified head of a dog flea, *Ctenocephalides canis*, colorized for effect.

inches from where they hatch. However, they do have a tendency to move away from light and heavy traffic—under furniture and behind doors are common places to find high quantities of flea larvae.

The flea larvae feed on dead organic matter, including adult flea feces, until they are ready to change into adult fleas. Fleas will usually remain as larvae for around seven days. After this period, the larvae will pupate into protective pupae. While inside the pupae, the larvae will undergo metamorphosis and change into adult fleas. This can take as little time as a few days, but the adult fleas can remain inside the pupae waiting to hatch for up to two years. The pupae are signaled to hatch by certain stimuli, such as physical pressure—the pupae's being stepped on, heat from an animal's lying on the pupae or

FLEA-KILLER CAUTION— "POISON"

Flea killers are poisonous. You should not spray these toxic chemicals on areas of a dog's body that he licks, including his genitals and his face. Flea killers taken internally are a better answer, but check with your vet in case internal therapy is not advised for your dog.

The dog flea is the most common parasite found on pet dogs.

S. E. M. BY DR. DENNIS KUNKEL, UNIVERSITY OF HAWAII.

increased carbon-dioxide levels and vibrations—indicating that a suitable host is available.

Once hatched, the adult flea must feed within a few days. Once the adult flea finds a host, it will not leave voluntarily. It only becomes dislodged by grooming or the host animal's scratching. The adult flea will remain on the host for the duration of its life unless forcibly removed.

Dwight R Kuhn's magnificent action photo, showing a flea jumping from a dog's back.

PHOTO BY DWIGHT R. KUHN

TREATING THE ENVIRONMENT AND THE DOG

Treating fleas should be a two-pronged attack. First, the environment needs to be treated; this includes carpets and furniture, especially the dog's bedding and areas underneath furniture. The environment should be treated with a household spray containing an Insect Growth Regulator (IGR) and an insecticide to kill the adult fleas. Most IGRs are effective against eggs and larvae; they actually mimic the fleas' own hormones and stop the eggs and larvae from developing into adult fleas. There are currently no treatments available to attack the pupa stage of the life cycle, so the adult insecticide is used to kill the newly hatched adult fleas before they find a host. Most IGRs are active for many months, while adult insecticides are only active for a few days.

When treating with a household spray, it is a good idea to vacuum before applying the product. This stimulates as many pupae as possible to hatch into adult fleas. The vacuum cleaner should also be treated with an insecticide to prevent the eggs and larvae that have been collected in the vacuum bag from hatching.

The second stage of treatment is to apply an adult insecticide to the dog.

EN GARDE: CATCHING FLEAS OFF GUARD!

Consider the following ways to arm yourself against fleas:

- Add a small amount of pennyroyal or eucalyptus oil to your dog's bath. These natural remedies repel fleas.
- Supplement your dog's food with fresh garlic (minced or grated) and an hearty amount of brewer's yeast, both of which ward off fleas.
- Use a flea comb on your dog daily. Submerge fleas in a cup of bleach to kill them quickly.
- Confine the dog to only a few rooms to limit the spread of fleas in the home.
- Vacuum daily...and get all of the crevices! Dispose of the bag every few days until the problem is under control.
- Wash your dog's bedding daily. Cover cushions where your dog sleeps with towels, and wash the towels often.

A LOOK AT FLEAS

Fleas have been around for millions of years and have adapted to changing host animals. They are able to go through a complete life cycle in less than one month or they can extend their lives to almost two years by remaining as pupae or cocoons. They do not need blood or any other food for up to 20 months.

They have been measured as being able to jump 300,000 times and can jump 150 times their length in any direction, including straight up. Those are just a few of the reasons why they are so successful in infesting a dog!

THE LIFE CYCLE OF THE FLEA

Egg

Larva

Pupa

Adult

A scanning electron micrograph of a dog or cat flea, *Ctenocephalides*, magnified more than 100x. This image has been colorized for effect.

Traditionally, this would be in the form of a collar or a spray, but more recent innovations include digestible insecticides that poison the fleas when they ingest the dog's blood. Alternatively, there are drops that, when placed on the back of the dog's neck, spread throughout the hair and skin to kill adult fleas.

INSECT GROWTH REGULATOR (IGR)

Two types of products should be used when treating fleas—a product to treat the pet and a product to treat the home. Adult fleas represent less than 1% of the flea population. The pre-adult fleas (eggs, larvae and pupae) represent more than 99% of the flea population and are found in the environment; it is in the case of pre-adult fleas that products containing an Insect Growth Regulator (IGR) should be used in the home.

IGRs are a new class of compounds used to prevent the development of insects. They do not kill the insect outright, but instead use the insect's biology against it to stop it from completing its growth. Products that contain methoprene are the world's first and leading IGRs. Used to control fleas and other insects, this type of IGR will stop flea larvae from developing and protect the house for up to seven months.

DO NOT MIX

Never mix flea-control products without first consulting your vet. Some products can become toxic when combined with others and can cause fatal consequences.

TICKS AND MITES

Though not as common as fleas, ticks and mites are found all over the tropical and temperate world. They don't bite, like fleas; they harpoon. They dig their sharp proboscis (nose) into the dog's skin and drink the blood. Their only food and drink is dog's blood. Dogs can get Lyme disease, Rocky Mountain spotted fever (in the US only), tick bite paralysis and many other diseases from ticks and mites. They may live where fleas are found and they like to hide in cracks or seams in walls. They are controlled the same way fleas are controlled.

The American dog tick, *Dermacentor variabilis*, may well be the most common dog tick in many geographical areas, especially those areas where the climate is hot and humid. Most

A brown dog tick, *Rhipicephalus sanguineus*, is an uncommon but annoying tick found on dogs.

PHOTO BY CAROLINA BIOLOGICAL SUPPLY/PHOTOTAKE.

The head of an American dog tick, *Dermacentor variabilis*, enlarged and colorized for effect.

PHOTO BY DR. DENNIS KUNKEL, UNIVERSITY OF HAWAII.

DEER-TICK CROSSING

The great outdoors may be fun for your dog, but it also is an home to dangerous ticks. Deer ticks carry a bacterium known as *Borrelia burgdorferi* and are most active in the autumn and spring. When infections are caught early, penicillin and tetracycline are effective antibiotics, but if left untreated the bacteria may cause neurological, kidney and cardiac problems as well as long-term trouble with walking and painful joints.

S. E. M. BY DR. ANDREW SPIELMAN/PHOTOTAKE.

dog ticks have life expectancies of a week to six months, depending upon climatic conditions. They can neither jump nor fly, but they can crawl slowly and can range up to 16 feet to reach a sleeping or unsuspecting dog.

Human lice look like dog lice; the two are closely related.

PHOTO BY DWIGHT R. KUHN.

MANGE

Mites cause a skin irritation called mange. Some mites are contagious, like *Cheyletiella*, ear mites, scabies and chiggers. Mites that infest ears are usually controlled with ivermectin,

which can only be administered by a vet, followed by Tresaderm at home. It is essential that your dog be treated for mange as quickly as possible because some forms of mange are transmissible to people.

Opposite page:
The American dog tick, *Dermacentor variabilis*, is probably the most common tick found on dogs. Look at the strength in its eight legs! No wonder it's hard to detach them.

OPPOSITE: S. E. M. BY DR. DENNIS KUNKEL, UNIVERSITY OF HAWAII.

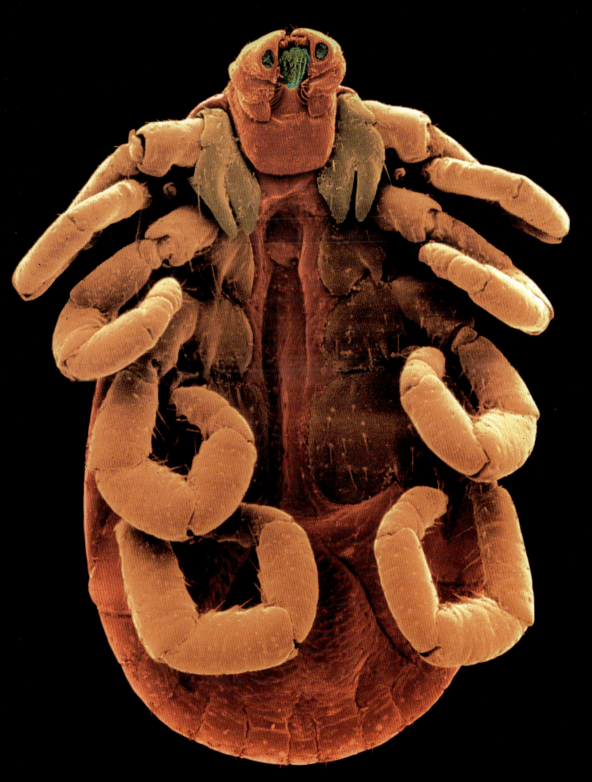

Photo by James Hayden/Yoav/Phototake

The mange mite, Psoroptes bovis.

INTERNAL PARASITES

Most animals—fishes, birds and mammals, including dogs and humans—have worms and other parasites that live inside their bodies. According to Dr. Herbert R. Axelrod, the fish pathologist, there are two kinds of parasites: dumb and smart. The smart parasites live in peaceful coopera-tion with their hosts (symbiosis), while the dumb parasites kill their hosts. Most worm infections are relatively easy to control. If they are not controlled, they weaken the host dog to the point that other medical problems occur, but they do not kill the host as dumb parasites would.

ROUNDWORMS

The roundworms that infect dogs are known scientifically as *Toxocara canis.* They live in the dog's intestines and shed eggs continually. It has been estimated that a dog produces about 6 or more ounces of feces every day. Each ounce of feces averages hundreds of thousands of roundworm eggs. There are no known areas in which dogs roam that do not contain roundworm eggs. The greatest danger of

ROUNDWORMS

Average-size dogs can pass 1,360,000 roundworm eggs every day. For example, if there were only 1,000,000 dogs in the world, the world would be saturated with thousands of tons of dog feces. These feces would contain around 15,000,000,000 roundworm eggs.

Up to 31% of home yards and children's sand boxes in the US contain roundworm eggs.

Flushing dog's feces down the toilet is not a safe practice because the usual sewage treatments do not destroy roundworm eggs.

Infected puppies start shedding roundworm eggs at three weeks of age. They can be infected by their mother's milk.

PHOTO BY CAROLINA BIOLOGICAL SUPPLY/PHOTOTAKE.

The roundworm *Rhabditis* can infect both dogs and humans.

roundworms is that they infect people too! It is wise to have your dog tested regularly for roundworms.

Pigs also have roundworm infections that can be passed to humans and dogs. The typical roundworm parasite is called *Ascaris lumbricoides.*

PHOTO BY DWIGHT R. KUHN.

DEWORMING

Ridding your puppy of worms is *very important* because certain worms that puppies carry, such as tapeworms and roundworms, can infect humans.

Breeders initiate deworming programs at or about four weeks of age. The routine is repeated every two or three weeks until the puppy is three months old. The breeder from whom you obtained your puppy should provide you with the complete details of the deworming program.

Your vet can prescribe and monitor the program of deworming for you. The usual program is treating the puppy every 15–20 days until the puppy is positively worm-free. It is advised that you only treat your puppy with drugs that are recommended professionally.

The common roundworm, *Ascaris lumbricoides.*

Left: The hookworm *Ancylostoma caninum.*

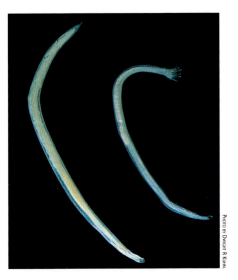

Right: Male and female hookworms.

HOOKWORMS

The worm *Ancylostoma caninum* is commonly called the dog hookworm. It is also dangerous to humans and cats. It has teeth by which it attaches itself to the intestines of the dog. It changes the site of its attachment about six times a day and the dog loses blood from each detachment, possibly causing iron-deficiency anemia. Hookworms are easily purged from the dog with many medications. Milbemycin oxime, which also serves as a heartworm preventative in Collies, can be used for this purpose.

In some regions, the "temperate climate" hookworm (*Uncinaria stenocephala*) is rarely found in pet or show dogs, but can occur in hunting packs, racing Greyhounds and sheepdogs because the worms can be prevalent wherever dogs are exercised regularly on grassland.

TAPEWORMS

There are many species of tapeworm, all of which are carried by fleas! The dog eats the flea and starts the tapeworm cycle. Humans can also be infected with tapeworms—so don't eat fleas! Fleas are so small that your dog could pass them onto your hands, your plate or your, food and thus make it possible for you to ingest a flea that is carrying tapeworm eggs.

The infective stage of the hookworm larva.

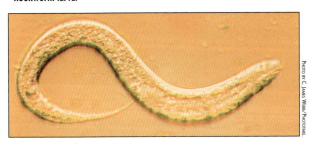

TAPEWORMS

Humans, rats, squirrels, foxes, coyotes, wolves and domestic dogs are all susceptible to tapeworm infection. Except in humans, tapeworms are usually not a fatal infection. Infected individuals can harbor 1000 parasitic worms.

Tapeworms, like some other types of worm, are hermaphroditic, meaning male and female in the same worm.

If dogs eat infected rats or mice, or anything carrying tapeworm, they get the tapeworm disease. One month after attaching to a dog's intestine, the worm starts shedding eggs. These eggs are infective immediately. Infective eggs can live for a few months without a host animal.

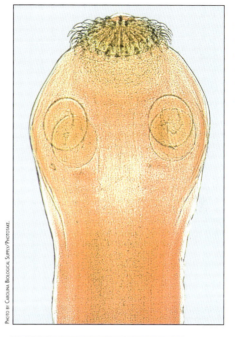

The head and rostellum (the round prominence on the scolex) of a tapeworm, which infects dogs and humans.

While tapeworm infection is not life-threatening in dogs (smart parasite!), it can be the cause of a very serious liver disease for humans. About 50% of the humans infected with *Echinococcus multilocularis*, a type of tapeworm that causes alveolar hydatis, perish.

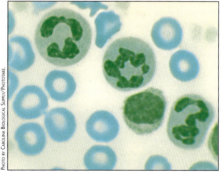

Magnified heartworm larvae, *Dirofilaria immitis.*

Heartworm, *Dirofilaria immitis.*

First Aid at a Glance

Burns
Place the affected area under cool water; use ice if only a small area is burnt.

Insect bites
Apply ice to relieve swelling; antihistamine dosed properly.

Animal bites
Clean any bleeding area; apply pressure until bleeding subsides; go to the vet.

Spider bites
Use cold compress and a pressurized pack to inhibit venom's spreading.

Antifreeze poisoning
Induce vomiting with hydrogen peroxide. Seek *immediate* veterinary help!

Fish hooks
Removal best handled by vet; hook must be cut in order to remove.

Snake bites
Pack ice around bite; contact vet quickly; identify snake for proper antivenin.

Car accident
Move dog from roadway with blanket; seek veterinary aid.

Shock
Calm the dog; keep him warm; seek immediate veterinary help.

Nosebleed
Apply cold compress to the nose; apply pressure to any visible abrasion.

Bleeding
Apply pressure above the area; treat wound by applying a cotton pack.

Heat stroke
Submerge dog in cold bath; cool down with fresh air and water; go to the vet.

Frostbite/Hypothermia
Warm the dog with a warm bath, electric blankets or hot water bottles.

Abrasions
Clean the wound and wash out thoroughly with fresh water; apply antiseptic.

 Remember: an injured dog may attempt to bite a helping hand from fear and confusion. Always muzzle the dog before trying to offer assistance.

HEARTWORMS

Heartworms are thin, extended worms up to 12 inches long, which live in a dog's heart and the major blood vessels surrounding it. Dogs may have up to 200 worms. Symptoms may be loss of energy, loss of appetite, coughing, the development of a pot belly and anemia.

Heartworms are transmitted by mosquitoes. The mosquito drinks the blood of an infected dog and takes in larvae with the blood. The larvae, called microfilariae, develop within the body of the mosquito and are passed on to the next dog bitten after the larvae mature. It takes two to three weeks for the larvae to develop to the infective stage within the body of the mosquito. Dogs are usually treated at about six weeks of age, and maintained on a prophylactic dose given monthly.

Blood testing for heartworms is not necessarily indicative of how seriously your dog is infected. This is a dangerous disease. Discuss the various preventatives with your vet, as there are many different types available. Together you can choose a safe course of prevention for your Presa Canario.

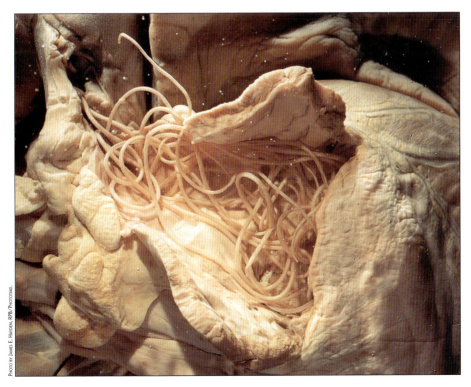

The heart of a dog infected with canine heartworm, *Dirofilaria immitis.*

HOMEOPATHY:
an alternative
to conventional
medicine

"Less is Most"

Using this principle, the strength of a homeopathic remedy is measured by the number of serial dilutions that were undertaken to create it. The greater the number of serial dilutions, the greater the strength of the homeopathic remedy. The potency of a remedy that has been made by making a dilution of 1 part in 100 parts (or 1/100) is 1c or 1cH. If this remedy is subjected to a series of further dilutions, each one being 1/100, a more dilute and stronger remedy is produced. If the remedy is diluted in this way six times, it is called 6c or 6cH. A dilution of 6c is 1 part in 1,000,000,000,000. In general, higher potencies in more frequent doses are better for acute symptoms and lower potencies in more infrequent doses are more useful for chronic, long-standing problems.

CURING OUR DOGS NATURALLY

Holistic medicine means treating the whole animal as a unique, perfect living being. Generally, holistic treatments do not suppress the symptoms that the body naturally produces, as do most medications prescribed by conventional doctors and vets. Holistic methods seek to cure disease by regaining balance and harmony in the patient's environment. Some of these methods include use of nutritional therapy, herbs, flower essences, aromatherapy, acupuncture, massage, chiropractic and, of course, the most popular holistic approach, homeopathy.

Homeopathy is a theory or system of treating illness with small doses of substances which, if administered in larger quantities, would produce the symptoms that the patient already has. This approach is often described as "like cures like." Although modern veterinary medicine is geared toward the "quick fix," homeopathy relies on the belief that, given the time, the body is able to heal itself and return to its natural, healthy state.

Choosing a remedy to cure a problem in our dogs is the difficult part of homeopathy. Consult with your vet for a professional diagnosis of your dog's symptoms. Often these symptoms require immediate conventional care. If your vet is willing, and knowledgeable, you may attempt a homeopathic remedy. Be aware that cortisone prevents homeopathic remedies from working. There are hundreds of possibilities and combinations to cure many problems in dogs, from basic physical problems such as excessive shedding, fleas or other parasites, unattractive doggy odor, bad breath, upset tummy, obesity, dry, oily or dull coat, diarrhea, ear problems or eye discharge (including tears and dry or mucousy matter), to behavioral abnormalities such as fear of loud noises, habitual licking, poor appetite, excessive barking and various phobias. From alumina to zincum metallicum, the remedies span the planet and the imagination…from flowers and weeds to chemicals, insect droppings, diesel smoke and volcanic ash.

Using "Like to Treat Like"

Unlike conventional medicines that suppress symptoms, homeopathic remedies treat illnesses with small doses of substances that, if administered in larger quantities, would produce the symptoms that the patient already has. While the same homeopathic remedy can be used to treat different symptoms in different dogs, here are some interesting remedies and their uses.

Apis Mellifica
(made from honey bee venom) can be used for allergies or to reduce swelling that occurs in acutely infected kidneys.

Diesel Smoke
can be used to help control travel sickness.

Calcarea Fluorica
(made from calcium fluoride, which helps harden bone structure) can be useful in treating hard lumps in tissues.

Natrum Muriaticum
(made from common salt, sodium chloride) is useful in treating thin, thirsty dogs.

Nitricum Acidum
(made from nitric acid) is used for symptoms you would expect to see from contact with acids, such as lesions, especially where the skin joins the linings of body orifices or openings such as the lips and nostrils.

Symphytum
(made from the herb Knitbone, *Symphytum officianale*) is used to encourage bones to heal.

Urtica Urens
(made from the common stinging nettle) is used in treating painful, irritating rashes.

My Perro de Presa Canario

PUT YOUR PUPPY'S FIRST PICTURE HERE

Dog's Name _____

Date _____ Photographer _____